Todd Lollis

BILLY GRAHAM

Personal
Thoughts
of a
Public
Man

BILLY GRAHAM

Personal Thoughts *of a* Public Man

30 years of conversations with

David Frost

Chariot VICTOR
PUBLISHING
A DIVISION OF COOK COMMUNICATIONS

Victor Books is an imprint of ChariotVictor Publishing
Cook Communications, Colorado Springs, CO 80918
Cook Communications, Paris, Ontario
Kingsway Communications, Eastbourne, England

BILLY GRAHAM: PERSONAL THOUGHTS OF A PUBLIC MAN
© 1997 by David Frost

Every effort has been made to trace copyright owners of material included in this book
listed in the chapter endnotes. We apologize for any inadvertent omissions or errors.

Cover and book design: Bill Gray
Cover photo: Eddie Adams Inc.
Back cover, page 178 photos: Ben Montanez
Research by Amanda Finkler, Paula Gerthe, Graham Scott
First printing, 1997
Printed in Canada
01 00 99 98 97   5 4 3 2

Library of Congress Cataloging-in-Publication Data

Frost, David.
        Billy Graham: personal thoughts of a public man/David Frost.
                p. cm.
        ISBN 0-7814-1545-4
        1. Graham, Billy, 1918—Interviews. 2. Evangelists—United States—Interviews.
3. Christianity—20th century. 4. Theology. 5. World politics—20th century. 6. Moral conditions. I. Title.
BV3785.G69F77 1997
269'.2'092—dc21
                                                                97-17191
                                                                CIP

Table of Contents

Preface

Introduction

Preface

The first time I ever interviewed Billy Graham on television was on BBC-2 in July 1964. I asked him what he regarded as the single most touching or moving demonstration of faith he had ever witnessed.

He responded: "I remember the opening night of our meeting in London in 1954, which you certainly remember. And the press was all against us. Every newspaper. The church leaders that had brought us there, many of them had deserted us. It had been brought up in Parliament as to whether I should even be allowed to land in Britian or not, and everything seemed against us. I had invited Senator Stuart Symington and another United States senator to be my special guests there. And that afternoon Senator Symington called me on the phone and said, 'The American ambassador feels that because of all this bad publicity that we should not come. Instead we're going to have dinner this evening with Sir Anthony Eden,' who was then the foreign secretary. And then I was called to my little hotel about a half an hour before the service, and they said, 'The place is empty. There are 400 newspaper people here taking pictures of all the empty seats.' And we had rented this place for three months.

"And so my wife and I got on our knees and said, 'Now, Lord, we're prepared for anything You want. It can be a total flop or it can be a success; we leave it in Your hands.' I had great peace about it. It was an exercise in faith to even go out there. We went out there. We didn't see a person. We got out of the car, and one of my associates came out of the door of the Harringay Arena and said, 'Billy, the place is packed, and there's 5,000 people on the other side trying to beat the doors down.' And I said, 'Where did they come from?' They said, 'We don't know; God must have sent them.' And we were there for three months, and not only did we not have empty seats, but we had two and three services a night on some nights to take care of the people and ended up at Wembley Stadium with the press all for us, the Archbishop of Canterbury sitting by my side."

In retrospect it hardly seems amazing that so many people showed up to hear the twentieth century's most powerful preacher, but at that time in 1954, in a country where Dr. Graham did not know what kind of a reception he would receive, I can understand why this was such an important faith-moment in his long ministry.

I can also understand why people came and why they came back again and again for three months. No one presented the Gospel of Jesus Christ as clearly or as straightforwardly as Dr. Graham. He believed his message totally, offered it without apology, and stated unequivocally how urgent he thought it was for people to accept Christ—now. And thousands responded. It was the same when I interviewed him on television in the sixties, seventies, eighties, and nineties. People responded.

Billy and I have had many conversations over the last thirty years. One day I was reviewing the tapes of the shows we have done together and it came to me that they comprised a record that should be put between the covers of a book, because of the permanence it would give his words. Television is a wonderful, powerful medium, but the words of Billy Graham merit the sort of additional study that is easiest in book form.

As I've compiled these interviews, reminisced, and added other comments I've come across, I have found it enormously interesting and satisfying. Not because it is a complete picture of Billy Graham's life and ministry—I doubt that any one book will ever be able to accomplish that—but because it gives a snapshot here and a snapshot there that together form a fascinating mosaic of evangelical Christianity as it attempted to hold its own in a century more known for its secular religions like fascism and communism.

I think the book is a unique summary of the man and his ministry and I recommend it to all who have been touched, inspired, guided, and/or blessed by Billy Graham.

David Frost
June 1997

Introduction

When David Frost's people approached us about publishing his television interviews with Billy Graham, we were intrigued. We remembered over the years how these two men—friends for over thirty years—fascinated audiences with their dialogues of faith. Frost asked the questions that were on millions of people's minds; Dr. Graham answered them without pretense or religiosity. If he didn't know the answer to some puzzling theological conundrum, Graham said so. If he had an opinion that was not rooted in the Bible, he qualified his answer.

If the answer was in Scripture, Graham put a spotlight on God's Word and gave his interpretation. Invariably, he would utter his trademark phrase, "The Bible says . . ." The television interviews made for grand viewing, and millions watched them here and abroad.

Our only question was the relevance of the interviews, that is, were they still timely? We should have known better from the start. In reviewing the tapes we found that far from being dated, they were more relevant now than ever. The Bible is a book for all people, and Billy Graham's focus for the whole of his ministry has been the ageless Word of God. Thus we knew we wanted to publish the Frost interviews as a way of giving historical permanence to them.

We are happy to add this book to the library of works that document the life and times of Billy Graham. Our prayer is that in some small way—like his ministry—it serves to glorify God.

The Publisher

Frost: What is the hymn that means the most to you?

Graham: You have a hymn in England that I first learned when I was there in the early fifties, *And Can It Be.*

Frost: "—that I should gain—"

Graham: "—that I should gain—"

Frost: "—An interest in the Savior's blood; died He for me who caused his pain, for me who Him to death pursued."

Graham: Good for you. That's the one that is my favorite hymn.

April 1997

CHAPTER 1

Billy Graham
on
Faith in God

I once asked Billy Graham what his goal was when he took the pulpit. He replied:

"First of all, I want the content to be accurate. I want it to be biblical, and I want it to be simple. I study to be simple."

I pressed him. "Can't a message be too simple?"

"When Dr. Karl Barth, the great Swiss theologian, the greatest theologian of his generation, was visiting America a couple of years ago, he was at one of our great seminaries, and a student asked him the question, 'Dr. Barth, what is the greatest single thought that ever crossed your mind?' And he bowed his head, and puffed on his pipe, and he slowly lifted his shaggy head, and they thought some tremendous statement was coming forth, and they were all on the edge of their seats, and he said,

'Jesus loves me, this I know,
For the Bible tells me so.' "

David Frost

*B*illy's own faith has never been complicated. In fact, he told me, he credits it to his simple upbringing. As he explained, he attended a Charlotte, North Carolina, revival meeting as a teenager, listened to an evangelist present the Gospel, and went forward to accept Christ as his Savior:

> **Graham:** When I was about sixteen, I went to hear an evangelist. I didn't know anything about evangelists. Our minister was somewhat opposed to that type of thing and we didn't know much about it. But this man stayed about eleven weeks, and on about the third week, I was taken to hear him. And something he said and some things he said, because all he did was just preach out of the Bible, spoke to my heart and I realized that I was a sinner. The moment that I went forward in that meeting, and that day in November 1934, was the time that I made my commitment.
>
> **Frost:** Not a great struggle then?
>
> **Graham:** I knew something had happened. I didn't know what. I don't think people saw any difference in my life. I remember going back to school the next day, high school, and the teacher made a little fun of me. She said, "I understand we have Preacher Graham with us today."[1]

He committed himself to full-time Christian service in spite of the fact that he had always said he didn't want to be a clergyman or an undertaker.[2] I listened as he told me about that pivotal walk on a golf course:

Graham: It was a full moonlight night that I'll never forget. I was walking by this eighteenth green, and it seemed to me that the Spirit of God just came into my heart in a tremendous surge of power. There were no tears; there were no lights flashing or anything like that. And I knelt down right there on the edge of that eighteenth green and I said, "Lord, I'll be what You want me to be and I'll do what You want me to do and I'll never change. . . ."

I didn't know at that time that I was going to travel around the world to seventy-five countries, preaching and meeting people of all kinds.[3]

Did his faith ever waver? Did he ever have any doubts? Yes, Billy honestly admitted, but not after a sylvan meeting with God. He told me:

Graham: I remember that I went out into the woods and I had my Bible with me, and on sudden impulse, I just opened the Bible. I don't know where I opened it to. And I said, "Lord, I don't understand all the things in this book, but I accept it as Your Word by faith. I can't prove it. There are things I don't understand. There are apparent contradictions here that I can't reconcile. There are things here, especially in the Old Testament, that I can't accept from my ethical and moral point of view today, but I accept it as Your revelation to us." And I've never had a doubt since then that the Bible is the Word of God.[4]

Billy restated his certainty. "I've never had doubts," he said. "Since my earliest days, from about 1950 on up, I've never doubted one time that the Gospel is true, the Bible is true, and that what I'm preaching is true.

"I think people are looking for authority. They want somebody who believes in something, and I really believe."[5]

And then on another occasion he reemphasized to me . . .

Graham: No, I really don't [have doubts], David. You may be surprised at that, but there was a time that I did. But I really don't have doubts, and if I did, I would tell you. These doubts have gone. I'm absolutely convinced if someone would come and give me a great deal of proof that the Bible was not true and Christ never lived, as some people say He didn't and so forth, this wouldn't disturb my faith at all because my faith is grounded in a personal encounter with Christ and a daily experience with Him. I know He lives. I know that He's the purpose and meaning of life. I know that He's the embodiment of truth. And to me, it's a tremendous sense of security that I have every day that I would like to pass on to every person I could.[6]

"What is the gift you've got?" I wondered.

Graham: I believe it's a gift of the Spirit of God, and when we get to heaven I'm going to reach over and grab David Frost—

Frost: Thank you. Thank you.

Graham: —if you're there—

Frost: Thank you.

Graham: —and I'll take you up to the Lord, and I'll say, "Now, David wants an answer to this question," because actually I cannot answer that. I'm as surprised as anyone else that this many people would come [to the crusades]. And I think the reason is . . . the world in which we're living is so uncertain with all of its frustration and confusion. And people read the tragic story, for example, of Judy Garland splashed all over the papers. And many people say, "Well, this is my story. I haven't yet gone this far, but this is the direction I'm taking. I need something." And I have become a symbol to many of these people that perhaps they can find in a spiritual experience with Christ the answer to their problems.

Frost: And I know one other thing. I'm going to knock at the gates of heaven and say, "Billy said I could come in. I'm going to—"

Graham: That won't do you any good. You've got to say, "Christ said I could come in."

Frost: Ah, yes. You've turned it to a good point there, yes. Tell me, what to you is an example of the most touching or moving demonstration of faith that you've ever witnessed? Is there one incident that you'd pick on and say, "Now, that is faith"?

Graham: I have had many such incidents happen in my life, and there are numerous occasions that have come up, but to say which is the most moving, one could take a small experience or one could take a large experience.

Frost: Take one of each.

Graham: I remember, for example, the opening night of our meeting in London in 1954, which you certainly remember. [7]

Billy then told the story I chose for the preface. But he was certainly right. I did remember that crusade well, because I had attended it as a teenager, when it had a great impact on me. I was at a watershed in my schoolboy life: getting in with what my parents would have called "bad company"; unsure about the existence of God, and about whether it mattered one way or the other anyway. . . . I do not want to be melodramatic, to portray Harringay as a Damascus experience. But it was certainly a Harringay experience. Somehow there was never any danger any more of my really going off the rails. And religion now engaged me intellectually in a way it had never done before.

After reminiscing about Harringay, I asked Billy to give us one small example of faith in action or someone with a touching faith. Here's what he told me:

Graham: One night in Los Angeles [in 1949], I was told that one of the leading criminals of this country was in the audience. [My committee] said, "We don't know why he's here. He may be here to be against you, or he may be here out of curiosity. We don't know why he's here." But they were trembling, my committee. We had a small tent and were preaching there on a street corner really. And that night this fellow was asked by an usher if he wanted to go forward when I gave the invitation. And he said, "If you speak to me again," he said, "I'll punch my—I'll take my fist and knock you down." But after about a minute or two, suddenly for some unknown reason, he decided to come forward.

Well, everybody in town thought this was a big hoax and a big fraud and it would never last, but I talked to him personally, and I believed he was sincere. He said, "I want you to go see my boss," who was Mickey Cohen, the great West Coast man, and I went out with him to see Mickey Cohen. I don't think Mickey Cohen had ever met a clergyman before, and he didn't know what to do. He said—he was very nervous, and he said, "What do you want to drink?' He said, "What does a person like you drink?" I said, "Well, give me a Coca-Cola." And so he got a Coca-Cola, and we talked for quite a while.

Well, the man who made the decision for Christ who was working for Mickey Cohen thought that he was going to get it because he had told Mickey Cohen that he was going to change his way of living and that he was going straight and going clean. Twenty years later, that fellow is doing social work in the city of New York and is one of the great Christian leaders of this city, and his name is Jim Voss, known to many people.

And the act of faith is this. Very few clergymen, very few people had any confidence in the commitment he had made. They thought he was just too bad to ever change. He never turned back one single day. He has lived it and is now making a positive contribution here in East Harlem for the work of God and for social improvement and betterment of this city.[8]

As an evangelist, Billy has tried to communicate his deep faith from the pulpit for more than fifty years. Ever since those early days in Los Angeles his goals have been consistent. Once he articulated them by saying, "First, we hope to win hundreds of people to a saving knowledge of the Lord Jesus Christ. There are thousands of lonely, discouraged, frustrated people who could find a new lease on life if they had an encounter with Christ. There are thousands who have a sense of guilt. There are others who have a sense of fear. This guilt and fear could be relieved by a personal faith in Jesus Christ. However, the Bible teaches as a result of sin, all of mankind is 'lost' from God. They need redemption.

"Second, revival in the church. Anyone studying the downward trend of statistics would have to admit that the church needs renewal, awakening and revival. It is our hope that this crusade will make at least a small contribution toward this end.

"Third, to give youth a challenge. . . . The crusades in America and in other parts of the world have grown as a result of the overwhelming interest of young people. Youth is searching for thrills and kicks. However, they also want an answer to the deepest problems of life. . . . They are deeply concerned about the basic issues of life and death. Many say they are bored; others have a sense of guilt; many testify that they are afraid of death; most of them wonder about God; most of them express a need to be loved. . . . I intend to direct a great deal of my preaching directly to young people. I am convinced that Jesus Christ has an answer to every question they are asking. The youth of today are tomorrow's leaders. Many of them are lost without any faith or philosophy of life at all. They want a faith to believe, a song to sing, and a flag to follow. I believe the greatest challenge in the world is serving Jesus Christ in the present world situation.

"Fourth, it is our hope to get millions talking and discussing—even arguing—religion. In other words, cause a religious stir. In the Book of Acts, wherever the apostles went there was a 'stir.' It is better than apathy.

"Fifth, to show that the Gospel of our fathers is relevant for modern problems whether they be individual or collective. God is not dead. The Gospel is not out of date. The Bible is not hard to understand. I am a twentieth-century man but I find the Bible thrilling and exciting. I find the Christian faith authoritative and exhilarating. I have personally experienced Christ. I want to share my faith with others.

"Sixth, it is our hope to encourage home prayer groups and Bible study groups. One church service a week is not enough. In the United States there are thousands of prayer groups and Bible study groups springing up throughout the nation. It is having an important effect on the spiritual life of the nation."[9]

And though I think the tone of his message has changed over the years, the heart of it has not. Billy states it best himself: "The message that the world needs and is hungering for is that *God is*. I don't think you have to spend much time trying to prove God today. . . .

"People today are hungry to know about God and it is wonderful when they hear that:

God loves them,

He is a person, and,

He is willing to forgive them.

"Almost everyone feels a sense of guilt; they don't know where the guilt comes from, but it's there, that something is out there somewhere—so many scientists are saying that now, especially since this big bang theory has come back into focus.

"When people realize that this God has come in the person of Jesus Christ and that you can experience in your own heart and life that He is real and He can be your friend every day, I think that this is a tremendous Gospel to preach.

"The word *gospel*, of course, means *good news* and that's good news to people who are suffering psychological and religious agonies—as most people are."[10]

Billy's unwavering belief in God has been clearly communicated throughout his ministry. I've asked presidents, politicians, and many others around the world, "Do you believe there's a God or do you know there's a God?" I wondered how Billy's answer would compare.

Bill Gates answered the question by saying, "I don't know if there's a God or not, but religious principles are quite valid,"[11] while author Salman Rushdie put it more bluntly: "I have never had a need for God. . . . I do not need the idea of God in order to explain the world I live in. In my view, I can do without it."[12] Ross Perot went a step further when he said, "I believe there's a God," but he didn't distinguish between believing and knowing.[13] In a similar vein, General Colin Powell answered the question this way: "I believe there is a God. I believe there is something beyond us, outside of us, there is something that has put this world here and put us here for a purpose."[14]

This was Billy's thought-provoking answer:

Graham: I know there is a God, but I cannot prove it scientifically. I think you can almost prove it, as many have said in the past, because you cannot look out at the stars and see the new discoveries they are making through these new telescopes without believing there's something there.

I talked to—one evening I had the privilege of sitting by her for two hours—Mrs. Gorbachev about three or four years ago. And, of course, she told me she was an atheist. But I had gone to the ambassador, [Anatoly] Dobrynin, whom I know very well, who was the ambassador to the United States. And I said to him that I was going to sit beside Mrs. Gorbachev. And I said, "What should I talk to her about?" and he said, "Talk to her about religion. That's what she's really interested in." Well, when it came my turn to be talking to her because she talked to the President first who was on the other side, she asked me what I did and I told her.

And she began to really ask me questions about philosophy and about religion and about the church and about God. Well, that led me straight to Christ and the cross and what I believed about salvation. But, it led me also to the fact that there is a God. And then she finally admitted, she said, "We know there is something up there bigger than we are." She said, "We may not call it God." But she said, "We know there is something bigger than we are." Well, she was telling me really that she was not really an atheist. And I've never met anyone in the world that I thought was a real atheist.

Frost: No one who was totally sure there wasn't a God?

Graham: That's right.[15]

"What's the nearest thing to proof that God exists?" I asked Billy in that same interview. His response:

Graham: The birth of a baby. I watched my youngest son being born. And the doctor that was delivering the baby looked up at me and he said, "How can anyone see this without realizing that there is a God?" He said, "Only God could bring all of this about." All of the preparation, the conception, the gestation, everything that goes into making a baby. And then how everything in the woman's body and the man's body is correlated to bring together the birth of a child. . . . Man couldn't do that. Evolution could have never come to that point. And to me, it's a very, it's a very obvious thing that there must be a God; there is a God.

Or, I look out at the stars and the moon and the sun. And I see that there are billions and trillions of these great planets and suns out in space, hundreds of Milky Ways bigger than ours and something is back of that, and everything moving in perfect precision. And the whole thing could blow up. But it doesn't, it keeps going. We see the sun come up in the morning and the sun set in the evening. We know that that's actually the world turning and so forth. We know so many things that we didn't know years ago. But something is there beyond man.[16]

Even in today's society, Billy still offers hope to those who are searching. He says, "Oh, I have tremendous hope, because I think the new interest in religion that's shown . . . indicates that American people are searching for something; they're not quite sure what, but they sum it up in the word *God*. I think that many millions of Americans are searching for God. And I think many are finding God in—in our various religions in this country."[17]

Finding God—that's a recurring theme in our discussions. His answer to the simple query, "How can I find God?" has been translated and distributed to millions around the globe: "To find God, the Bible teaches these simple steps. Believe that God is. Realize that

God loves you. Understand that God's love found expression in the giving of His Son, Jesus Christ, to die for mankind. Accept Jesus' sacrifice as washing away your guilt—no matter how you have misspent your years. Finally, commit your whole self to Him.

"If you take these steps, you will find God.

"Attending church, paying tithes, and doing good are only part of the Christian commitment, and the lesser part at that. The essence of the Christian life lies in the words that Jesus spoke to history's early God-seekers: 'You must be born again.' A thousand religious 'exercises' are as nothing without the miracle of rebirth in Christian love."[18]

Finally, on the subject of faith, I asked, "Do you want people to believe that the Bible is literally true from beginning to end?"

Graham: I would like them to believe that the Bible has been inspired of God. That it's God's message to us to help us in the direction of our lives. To help us in our decision about salvation. And to do the things that He tells us and He wants us to do in our daily lives. For example, the Great Commission: "Go ye into all the world and preach the Gospel." That's my orders from God—to keep proclaiming the Gospel.

The mistake that many make is that they worship the Bible. The Bible becomes sort of a fetish and we have it in our homes. A lot of people wouldn't have a home unless they had a Bible in it. But they never look at the Bible. So the Bible is just disregarded as far as they are concerned. It means nothing to them. It's sort of a fetish to have that, sort of an icon.

I believe that the Bible was inspired by God. And this is

what God would have us, now, to do, and how to live and how to be saved and so forth is in the Scriptures. And it's a book that is also a book about the future. People are worried today about the future. The whole future is unraveled in the Bible. It's right there to be seen.[19]

Endnotes

1. "A Prophet with Honor: David Frost Documentary on Billy Graham," Channel Four, Great Britain, 1989.

2. Harris, Kenneth. "Meet Billy Graham." *The Christian Herald and Signs of Our Times*, June 10, 1966, 15.

3. "A Prophet with Honor: David Frost Documentary on Billy Graham," Channel Four, Great Britain, 1989.

4. *Ibid*.

5. *20/20*, Interview with Billy Graham, December 20, 1970.

6. "Doubts and Certainties: David Frost interview with Billy Graham," BBC-2, 1964.

7. "The David Frost Show: Interview with Billy Graham." July 1969.

8. "Doubts and Certainties: David Frost interview with Billy Graham," BBC-2, 1964

9. "Dr. Graham has the answers (and questions) all ready." *The Christian and Christianity Today*, May 27, 1966, 14.

10. "Hello Billy." *Christian Herald*, London: February 23, 1980.

11. "Bill Gates Talking with David Frost," PBS, November 24, 1995.

12. "Salman Rushdie Talking with David Frost," PBS, November 26, 1993.

13. "Ross Perot Talking with David Frost," PBS, April 4, 1992.

14. "General Colin Powell Talking with David Frost," September 29, 1995.

15. "Reverend Billy Graham Talking With David Frost," PBS, January 29, 1993.

16. *Ibid*.

17. *Today Show*, Interview with Billy Graham, April 1, 1994.

18. Graham, Billy. "Some Tormenting Questions for Our Time." *Reader's Digest*, April 1972.

19. "Reverend Billy Graham Talking with David Frost," PBS, January 29, 1993.

CHAPTER 2

Billy Graham
on
Family and Marriage

My father, away from home so much of the time, left most of the responsibilities and burdens of rearing five children to my mother . . . when he was home, he led us in daily Bible reading and prayer. How precious it was to have him take his role as spiritual leader seriously. He practiced at home what he preached in public. Children need to see fathers on their knees, acknowledging and bowing to a higher authority, and loving their mother.

Gigi Graham Tchividjian
Passing It On

*B*illy and Ruth Graham married on August 13, 1943. Billy has said he "married the most wonderful woman in the whole world. I saw her walking across the campus. . . . I fell in love with her right then. . . . It took me a month to get up enough courage to ask her for a date because she was so beautiful and so—she had come from China, and she was a very spiritual woman. She got up every morning at four to pray. That impressed me tremendously."[1] Ruth, raised in China by missionary parents, had planned to return there as a missionary following her schooling. Billy, on the other hand, did not feel called by God to China. In that context, Billy's been quoted as saying at that time about where they would serve, "God will lead me, and you will do the following."[2] In those days, women's place in society was behind the scenes. Knowing the Grahams as I do, it seems the dynamic of their marriage has evolved considerably over the years.

Some time ago Billy Graham said, "A marriage should be made up of three people: you, your spouse, and God. Christ should be the foundation of a Christian marriage right from the beginning. A lasting marriage starts during courtship. I would say to a young person who is beginning to think about marriage: 'Yield this whole area of your life to Christ, and trust Him. Don't take your cue from the world: realize that marriage is a lifetime commitment. You shouldn't go into it with the idea you can always get out of it if things don't work out. And realize that true love is not selfish.' "[3]

When I asked Billy what it takes to make a marriage work, he expanded on this basic premise of self-sacrificial love.

> **Frost:** You and your wife are a terrific example of how to stay in love. What would you say makes a marriage work?
>
> **Graham:** I think to have a successful marriage you need two very good forgivers. They have to learn to forgive each other. And I think the most difficult period of marriage is probably the first five years of adjustment. That's very difficult. After about five years there develops an understanding so that a couple can communicate with each other without ever saying a word. And I know that in my own case I suppose it's been at least fifteen years since my wife and I have had a cross word between us. I mean, we think alike, we believe alike, and we desperately love each other. I love her far more now than I did when I married her. And I believe she loves me.
>
> And also learning to accept the faults of each other. I think that Abraham Lincoln was right when he said, "I've learned to accept the faults of my friends." And I think you can establish a friendship or marriage relationship when you learn to realize that no one is perfect, that we do have little faults.
>
> And then thirdly I think—and basically there must be spiritual affinity. There must be something more than the physical or the material. There must be a spiritual understanding in a marriage. And if there isn't this spiritual oneness and understanding, I think the marriage is in danger, because it must have a strong rock upon which to build. And, of course, when two people can face a problem as we all have and can pray about it and talk about it in a spiritual

dimension and face it that way, of course their possibility of settling that problem is far greater.[4]

On the same topic Billy has also said, "Many marriages end by the fifth year because couples haven't learned how to adjust. Differences can be settled amicably if both are really seeking the Lord's will. One of the things Ruth and I have found helpful is that when we kneel to pray together, she prays for me and my problems and I pray for her and her problems or concerns.

"A man especially needs to learn to be extremely gentle. A woman must have tenderness from her spouse; she can love him and respond to him if he is tender—no matter what he looks like or whether or not he is successful. . . . We need to learn to say, 'I was wrong; I'm sorry.' And we also need to say, 'That's all right; I love you.' "[5]

Our discussion back in 1970 on what makes a marriage work led to a discussion of the women's liberation movement—a very timely issue that year—and the evangelist's definition of love.

Frost: Do you have much sympathy with the women's liberation movement?

Graham: Well, in the December issue of *The Ladies' Home Journal* I have several thousand words on the subject. And I suppose that I'm going to get a lot of letters on my article because I—actually I wrote the article and I submitted it to my wife because she's a marvelous critic, and she handed it back to me all blue penciled and said, "I don't agree with most of this." So I rewrote it, so that what I've written is partially what my wife believes. I did say that woman didn't have much of a chance in the world until Jesus came along and that with His liberation He gave a liberation of the spirit. . . .

Frost: So that in general you think women are missing the point a bit?

Graham: Yes, I think so. I think that when it comes to equal pay for equal work and all of that, I think there's a big point that they do have, and I'm in sympathy with them. But some of these other rather ridiculous things—for example, I saw one group, and they said that they wanted even the signs on the restrooms taken down. Well, that is extreme, silly, ridiculous.

Frost: You mentioned love just now when talking about marriage. What would be your definition of love between a man and a woman?

Graham: I think the love between a man and a woman is described very accurately by the Apostle Paul in the thirteenth chapter of 1 Corinthians, in which he says that love is patient and love never gets angry and love does not hold grudges and so forth. I think that in order to have successful married love, we have to work at it. You know we've got the idea that love is some sort of sensual feeling, or we've got the idea that love is something that sort of hits you. And I've got a feeling that love grows, and I'm sure that when I got married that I didn't really love my wife in the depths that I'm able to love her now, or that she loved me. We called it love, but there's a great gap between that little puppy love that we started with and what I believe to be a gigantic Rock of Gibraltar love that we have now. . . . But that's taken work.

Frost: What's the difference between that love, your love for your wife, and your love for your children or your love for your God? How do they differ?

Graham: There are three words in Greek that are translated *love*. One is *eros*, which is sexual love or sensuous love. The other is *philia* love, which is friendship love, the type of love that I would have for a friend. The other is *agape* love, and that love is God's love. And the New Testament writers had to invent a brand new word. It did not exist in Greek. They invented a new word to describe God's love, which is total love—God's love for us. For example, even when we were sinners and rebellious against God, He loved us anyway, so much so that He gave His Son to die on the cross for us. That's God's love. Now, the moment I receive Christ as my Savior, God gives me the gift of that love. I have an ability to almost supernaturally love, so that the love that I have in my marriage between two Christians is a love that is almost a supernatural love. It is a supernatural love. There's a depth to it. There's a joy to it. There's an excitement, even an ecstasy that I don't think a person outside of God knows about.[6]

More recently I asked Billy, "Are you as in love as you were the day you married? Or is it a different form of love, or what?"

Graham: It's both. I'm more deeply in love. We know each other better. We love each other more. We communicate with each other even though we don't talk. It's something that's very difficult to explain. And I think that true love comes from God. And I think that a marriage must consist of three people: the man, the woman, and God. And if God has brought you together, then there's going to be Someone to turn to. Because every marriage has its difficulties. I don't care if it's Billy Graham's marriage or whose marriage, there's going to be difficulties. We have had our . . . not arguments, I would say, but we've come close to it. And we've had many of our differences. We still have differences. Not as many as we did for years. It takes time to adjust. But when you travel as much as I do, and am away from home, we have to readjust every time we get back together. It's both a honeymoon, and it's also a readjustment period, and we have to get some things straightened out when we come home.

And then, of course, in any marriage, there's always the financial problem. When I asked her father for her hand in marriage, when he finally came home from China, he said, "Well, I have two daughters. One is a spender and one is a saver. You've asked for the spender." Which didn't mean much in those days or any day in our marriage, but to an extent, we have had those type of difficulties. Because Ruth would give everything away. I mean, she just gives to any poor person, any sick person, any person who needs any help, she's there.

Frost: Which is the stronger love in your life: the love of God or the love of Ruth and the children?

Graham: The love of God. But I don't think you can separate them because I think God gave me Ruth and gave me the children. And I love them all.

Frost: In the perfect marriage, in the marriage blessed by God, as you say, all those loves intermingle?

Graham: They do, indeed.

Frost: But there must have been times in your life when you had to choose between what you thought God was asking you to do and what Ruth and the family would have felt would have been better?

Graham: Yes, there have been times like that. There were times when I was called to preach in some foreign country that was going to take me away a long time, and Ruth thought that I ought to be home, or the children thought the same thing. And I made the choice to go and do what I thought God wanted me to do. And then the moment I make that choice, Ruth is backing me 100 percent. I've never known her one time to say, "Stay home. Don't go. . . ." If God has called you, you obey God.[7]

I'm touched by the depth of the relationship between Billy and Ruth. She has been a consummate team player in the ministry of her husband, who has said he couldn't have accomplished what he has without her. Once he revealed: "When my wife left me yesterday, I broke down and cried. I just couldn't bear to think of being three or four weeks without her. That represents a real change in our lives. Up until a few years ago we were so used to coming and going that we didn't think much about it. But now all five of our children are on their own, so there are only the two of us, and we have become very dependent upon each other. Ruth contributes to me emotionally and intellectually, and I do to her, in ways I never dreamed two people of our age would rely on each other."[8]

Billy set the record straight as to just how important his wife is to him in this exchange, one of my favorites:

Frost: Billy, I know that material possessions and so on—things don't matter too much to you. . . . But if there was a burglar who somehow got into your house, but he said he'd leave you one material possession or gift you've ever received if you asked him nicely or whatever, what would you say you wanted to keep?

Graham: My wife. I hope she's watching.

Frost: Would it all have been possible without your wife, in fact, do you think?

Graham: No. My wife, David, you must know—David and I have been friends for a number of years. But you must know her because she is an unusual person. She rarely ever changes temperament. Her temperament is the same all the time—very sweet and very gracious and very charming and a great student of the Bible. Her life is ruled more by the Bible than any person I've ever known. That's her rule book, her compass. And she reared our children, our five children, with a Bible in one hand and a switch in the other, and they've turned out pretty well.[9]

Billy's comment about Ruth's rearing their children reminded me of a quote I once read about their family. He said, "I have a very remarkable wife that God must have sent. She was born and raised in China and sent to school in North Korea. She was used to danger and toughness. She took our three daughters and two sons and said, 'You go preach the Gospel, and I'll raise these children for God and you'll be proud of them when they grow up.' When I did come home, my children knew they came first."[10]

And he knew how he wanted them to turn out, as he expressed when he said, "I don't care what my children or grandchildren do in life, they can become newspaper people, or photographers, or ditch diggers, or college presidents, just so they love the Lord."[11]

I recall a television interview in which Billy offered advice for rearing children in a world filled with immorality. As he attests, this formula certainly had good results in his own family. "Be available to your children at all times, if possible, especially in their formative years and secondly, love your children. You know, a psychiatrist said something many years ago at Columbia University I never forgot. He said, if your child goes through a period of rebellion in adolescence, always keep the love of that child and when they come through it as they will, at some point usually, the love will be intact. Let them know you disapprove but don't argue and debate and fight with your child and make the child angry. And, they'll come through and I believe the love will prevail.

"We all face the same thing with our children. I have five children and thank God they've all come through it and they're all happily married and they all love the Lord. And some of them are Bible teachers. And several are in Christian work which I am happy to say."[12]

"Can you think of any occasion—circumstance—whereby it would be okay for a parent to just give up on a child or abandon a child?" he was asked. Knowing what he and Ruth went through with one of their sons, his answer is telling:

"No, I certainly do not. I don't think that any parent can do that really in his heart or especially a mother if she's a real mother."[13]

I remembered that Billy was away from home when his first child was born and asked him about that.

Graham: I was [away on a preaching trip]. . . and I was wrong, because my wife had asked me to stay home. She said, "I think the baby is going to come in the next week or two and I think you should be home." And I said, "I think I should be home, too, but I don't think the baby is coming that quick." But the baby did come while I was away, and that's one of the regrets of my life. I came back, and, of course, kissed my wife and hugged her and apologized and tried to apologize to the little baby. And the little baby doesn't live far from where you and I are now and she has eight children of her own and she has ten grandchildren, and that's that little baby and she's a marvelous woman married to a marvelous man.

Frost: How many grandchildren do you have?

Graham: We have, I think, about twenty-two now.

Frost: At the last count?

Graham: At the last count.[14]

On a lighter note, Billy revealed this glimpse of his family's Christmas celebration to me one year. I include it because it's such a happy snapshot of the Graham's family life. This "snapshot" was taken during a London interview we did in 1970.

Graham: This year is going to be a little bit different than we've spent in other years, because we have to leave the day after Christmas to go to California, where Ruth and I are the grand marshals of the Rose Parade this year. And so this means that we're going to have to hurry Christmas along. We'll have a lot of our family with us, we hope all of our family, and then we're going to put them all in a plane and take the whole crowd out to California, where we will be involved in about a weeklong series of festivities climaxing with the Rose Parade and the Rose Bowl and so forth.

I have done most of my Christmas shopping in two hours at one of the stores in London while I was here, and I bought all of my children little presents and bought my wife a couple things. I would tell you what I bought her, but she might see this before Christmas, so I can't reveal it, you see. But I did have quite a good time doing this Christmas shopping.

Then on Christmas Eve, we always hang up stockings for everybody, and we put our presents in there. And then we gather and have hymn singing and carol singing and prayers, as we do every evening in our home—we have prayers. Christmas morning we get up rather early, keeping the tradition of the little children when they used to wake us up early, and we have oyster stew for some strange reason—and my wife and I are about the only two that seem to like it. But she wrote a book one time on Christmas, and she put that in, that we did that, so she has to keep it up every year, even though very few like it. And then Christmas lunch we always have the traditional turkey. And then in the afternoon we try to sleep it off.

Frost: What? The oyster stew mainly?

Graham: That's right. The oyster stew is beginning to gurgle a bit by that time, and the oysters are swimming about. But, seriously, Christmas to us is not much of a commercial thing. It's a family occasion, and it's a time when we try to remember very seriously what Christmas is all about. A lot of people forget that.[15]

Endnotes

1. *Larry King Live*, Interview with Billy Graham, January 21, 1997.

2. "The Preacher's Wife: Women Who Marry Preachers." *People Weekly*, February 10, 1997, 162.

3. "Candid Conversation with the Evangelist." *Christianity Today*, July 17, 1981, 18.

4. "The David Frost Show," Westinghouse Broadcasting, 1970.

5. "Candid Conversation with the Evangelist." *Christianity Today*, July 17, 1981.

6. "The David Frost Show," Westinghouse Broadcasting, 1970.

7. "Reverend Billy Graham Talking with David Frost," PBS, January 29, 1993.

8. Beam, James Michael. "I Can't Play God Any More." *McCall's*, January 1978, 100.

9. "The David Frost Show," Westinghouse Broadcasting, 1969.

10. Rowan, Ray. "In His Own Words." *People Weekly*, December 22, 1975.

11. *20/20,* Interview with Billy Graham, December 20, 1979.

12. *Donahue*, Interview with Billy Graham, November 1979.

13. *Ibid.*

14. "Reverend Billy Graham Talking with David Frost," PBS, May 30, 1997.

15. "The David Frost Show," Westinghouse Broadcasting, 1970.

CHAPTER 3

Billy Graham
on
Politics

Billy Graham has no hidden agendas. Billy Graham is not an emissary for any government. He's not an emissary for any organization. He's only an emissary for Christ.

Senator Mark Hatfield

I once asked Billy if there were any questions the evangelist would want to ask God when he got to heaven. Billy's answer included a surprising admission.

> **Graham:** I'm going to ask Him, "Lord, why did you choose me to do this particular work?" Because I've never really understood how I was chosen to go around the world preaching to these great crowds of people. And I'm humbled by it and honored by it, but it's not the life I personally would have chosen. I think this was chosen by God and He gave me this privilege and this opportunity, and I want to ask Him when there are so many wonderful people in the world that are His servants why He chose me.

> **Frost:** If he hadn't chosen you to be a evangelist, what might you have chosen to be?

> **Graham:** I probably would have gone into politics. Politics fascinates me.[1]

Billy has said he has "serious reservations about religious groups getting involved in partisan politics or saying 'God is for us.' . . . Lincoln said, 'I'm not so concerned as to whether God is on my side or not, but I am concerned as to whether I'm on God's side or not.'"[2] However his concern has not prevented him from some involvement in politics.

"Weren't you considered as a candidate for president in 1964?" I asked.

> **Graham:** Briefly, until my father-in-law called and my

wife called and said, "If you announce that you're going to run for president," she said, "I'll divorce you and America will not elect a divorced man."

Frost: But it was there for a moment?

Graham: It was there for a moment, and telegrams were coming in from people who said that they would pledge their delegates to me, and so forth and so on. And interestingly, it was the Republicans, and I'm a Democrat![3]

I also know that he has been offered several positions by presidents. Nixon offered him any job he wanted; Johnson offered him the ambassadorship to Israel. In response to that offer, he told Golda Meir, "I am not the man. God has called me to preach." In fact with Johnson he was much more blunt: "The Middle East would blow up if I went over there."[4]

Back in 1969, he went on to tell me how he came to have the political influence he has:

Graham: I have happened to be friends with two or three men who became president years later after our friendship began. I knew Mr. Johnson for many years, and I knew Mr. Nixon for many years. I knew his father and mother back as far as 1949. And then he became senator after that and then vice president, and through the years our friendship grew. And he told me many times, "Billy, at all costs you stay out of politics." In 1960 he said, where there was some pressure on me to endorse him and I had no intention of getting into politics if I could avoid it, but he told me at that time—he said, "Your ministry is more important than my election." And this has been his attitude.

Frost: President Nixon, in fact, publicly gave you part of the credit for persuading him to run again [in 1968], didn't he?

Graham: Yes. I don't know whether he did or whether somebody quoted him or not. I've never really discussed it with him. But when he was trying to make up his mind as to whether or not to run, he invited me to come down to Florida and spend a few days with him, because I had been in bed with pneumonia. And he said, "Come down and breathe some of this good air and get some sunshine and we'll have some talks." So I went down and stayed with him, and we discussed many things and watched a football game and so forth.

I gave him the reasons why I thought any prominent American in whom many people had confidence ought to offer himself at a critical period of history—not specifically him, but any American. That was more or less the way we left it. Whether that had any influence in his decision or not, I don't really know . . . because he's never told me.

Frost: I've read several accounts of your involvement in the choice of Vice President Agnew. What's the truth about that one?

Graham: The *New York Times* has carried the truth about that. . . . In June [1968] they carried a story in the magazine section on me, and they were accurate at this point. I went up that evening after Mr. Nixon's nomination to congratulate him at his hotel, and he said, "We're going to talk about the vice president, which is a very important decision to make tonight." And he said, "I think you'd find it interesting to listen." So I went into the room, and there were these Republican leaders, and I must confess I felt a little ill at ease. But I was interested also, as anyone would be curious, to hear how these things are done.

Mr. Nixon went right around the room and asked every-one of these leaders to give his position. And did you know that I never heard the name *Agnew* mentioned all evening? Never heard it mentioned except by one person, a New Yorker, and he was not recommending him. And I certainly never heard Senator [Strom] Thurmond mention his name—as some people have said that he was the one that chose him. That was not true at all.

And when this was done and how it was done, it was certainly done after about four in the morning when I left and the others left. I don't know how that came about, and I've never asked the president how this came about.

Frost: But that evening did the president ask you your view? He did, didn't he?

Graham: Yes, he did. He turned to me last and asked me my view, and I felt at that time that he needed a balance, what I thought a balance, to the ticket, and I gave him a recommendation which, of course, everybody knows he didn't take.

Frost: Your recommendation was Mark Hatfield, wasn't it?

Graham: Senator Mark Hatfield, yes, because Senator Hatfield is a very dedicated Christian and holds different views on some issues than Mr. Nixon, and I thought it might give balance to the ticket. [5]

In 1968, Billy stated publicly that he had voted for Nixon. When asked if he had second thoughts about revealing this, he said that although he is a Democrat, he thought Nixon was the better qualified man, and he had been a friend of Richard Nixon's for more than twenty years.[6]

Some have suggested that Billy's relationships like this one and his relationship with other political leaders has been too cozy. I reminded him of this.

> **Frost:** People say that Jesus was at odds with the political leaders of His time. He was condemning them. It was an adversary relationship and yours is not; Jesus' [relationship] would have been different.

> **Graham:** It has been adversarial in private. A number of things I have completely disagreed, and argued a point of view that they didn't particularly accept. But I haven't done it in public because I knew if you do it in public, you never get an opportunity to do it again. I have been asked advice by politicians from time to time, and I've given them exactly what I think I should give them, if that's my conviction. Some of them, they ask questions I don't know the answer to, and I just tell them I don't have an opinion on that.

> **Frost:** Do politicians ask more for advice or for a blessing on their endeavors?

> **Graham:** Advice. I don't think I've ever sensed that one wanted a blessing on what he was doing or saying.[7]

In a 1989 retrospective, I broached the subject of Watergate and Nixon.

> **Frost:** You got very close to Richard Nixon and then the whole Watergate business was an embarrassment, wasn't it?

> **Graham:** It was a warm friendship, and I have great admiration for Mr. Nixon. How Watergate came to be, I don't know. It was an amazement to me and a shock to me and a disappointment to me, but I remember that one of the men on the investigating committee told me, the chairman

told me, that he listened to hours of those tapes and he said that there came a time when it seemed that somebody else took over, and he wondered if I would think that might have been the Devil.

I said, "I don't know, but it might be," because it didn't sound like Mr. Nixon, and it wasn't him at all. And the words that he used, I never knew he even knew those words because I'd been with him many times and he was always the perfect gentleman and is today.

Frost: So it could have been the Devil?

Graham: It could have been. I mean, I couldn't answer that for sure, but I think he was caught in something that was beyond his ability to handle.[8]

Billy once told me that he had forebodings about President Kennedy going to Dallas, and he shared with others his feelings that something dreadful was going to happen.

Graham: I called George Smathers, who had been in his [Kennedy's] wedding and who was a close friend of mine, ... and I said, "George, I don't think that the president ought to go to Texas at this time." I said, "The tension is pretty high down there about him and some of his policies." He said, "Well, I'll pass that on to him." But I don't think that he ever did.

All the presidents that I have met, I knew them before they ever became president. That's the interesting thing. And I spent more time with Johnson than any other president because he wanted a minister around him all the time.[9]

And the mention of Lyndon Johnson's name naturally segued us into a discussion about America's involvement in Vietnam. I knew that the situation there had torn at Graham's soul, as his biographer William Martin has said.[10]

> **Graham:** Going to Vietnam two or three times myself and seeing the impossibility of it, however we got involved in that war, I'll never know. And while our motives might have been good as Americans—I'm speaking about Americans and not Christians now—they might have been good in the beginning, we got bogged down in something that anybody that would go into Vietnam or go into Asia would get bogged down in.
>
> **Frost:** What's the lesson of that, of the Vietnam War?
>
> **Graham:** I think one of the big lessons is that we should do more talking and less fighting. I think that the world is ready for strong leadership on disarmament.[11]

Chuck Colson once admitted that the prayer breakfasts and worship services Billy Graham participated in during Nixon's administration were used for political purposes.[12] I wondered if Graham ever felt used by politicians or their aides.

> **Graham:** Yes. By several of them. By the aides. I never felt used by the politician himself so much, never really, because I saw them privately. And I never had been to the Oval Office in all these years more than two or three times. I always see them in their private quarters and become family friends.
>
> **Frost:** Where you have felt used, how were you used?
>
> **Graham:** I couldn't answer that. I remember—I just

don't believe that the president, presidential candidate or the president himself, has ever attempted to use me.[13]

In a later interview, I asked Graham again about the perils of being a friend of political leaders and serving God's purposes at the same time.

Graham: Not now so much as in the earlier years before I knew better. Today, that's not a problem at all. It's God and God alone that I serve. I will be a friend to men of both parties, but I would never say that I was, even indicate that I was for one or the other. I am for God. I don't think there's any hope for the world except in God. I don't think any . . . I think the job's too big for any president, or any man, and I think the same is true in many parts of the world. They can't govern the world. This country can't be governed, I don't think, by one many, or by a group of people. I think only God working through these men is going to be. . . . That's the reason it's so important for us to have prayer groups and prayer meetings and join hands together, whether we're Protestant, Catholics, or Jews, and pray, because we are praying to the same God.

Frost: Do you think there was a time when you were perhaps beguiled by being "shoulder to shoulder" with the presidents and the powerful men of the world? Do you think that was a sort of tempting, a beguiling experience?

Graham: I'm not sure, David. I've often thought about that. Always, in the back of my mind, I said, "This is a way to serve God, not only to influence them spiritually, and religiously, but to influence the people that they influence." And secondly that this is a voice that they don't hear. Very few people will tell the president about spiritual things and religious things or have prayer with him, and I felt that this was a way that God used me, and I felt I was a servant of God when I was with these people.

Frost: What do all these presidents, all these people with power have in common?. . . What lessons have you drawn? What . . . are the responsibilities of power?

Graham: I think that many of them go after this thing because of ego. I think some go after it because they really feel that they can make a great contribution to the country that they serve. But, I think that once they get into the position, a great transformation takes place. They become either tired or humbled by it, or changed by it. They are not so cocksure that they've got all the answers.

I'm an admirer, for example, of a certain prime minister right now, and I had a time with him a few weeks ago and he is totally different in person than he is in the press. And, he is a man that has a tremendous intellect. . . . He reminds me of MacArthur or Churchill. And I think that there are people like that and they have a lot to offer.

But many people, I think, in this country, are pulling back from politics because they don't want their lives investigated to the nth degree and their families embarrassed, and all that goes with politics today. I think we are in danger of losing some of the great people that we've got in this country for the future because of the investigative reporting that's gone so far and I think that sort of began with Watergate.[14]

More than once I asked Billy if it was possible he was too much of a political insider, instead of a rebel, a disturber of the peace—like Jesus. In answering that question, he explained Jesus' politics, his own rub with churches that don't take a strong position on the race question, and why Russia fell apart in 1917.

Frost: People point out sometimes that in Jesus' time He seemed to be very much against the system. He was outside of the system, and He was opposed to the system and He was, in a sense, a rebel against the system. At the same time today you are a great friend of a lot of the men within the system. . . . What is your answer to people who say you ought to be against the system, you ought to be like Jesus?

Graham: We have to understand what Jesus was against. He never did say one word against Rome, and Rome ruled the world, including the country He came from. He never said a word against Rome. He was against the religious system, and He dealt primarily with religious questions. And when they tried to trap Him and tried to get Him to say that He gave allegiance to Caesar or He was against Caesar, He said, "Bring me a coin." And He said, "Whose picture is on that?" And they said, "Caesar." He said, "Render unto Caesar the things that are Caesar's and unto God the things that are God's." He made that distinction, and He never said anything against Rome. The system He was against was an evil, corrupt religious—hypocritical religious system.

Now I make pretty strong statements against some of what I believe to be the theological and moral corruption that we have in certain areas of the church today. . . . If I go to some area where the church has not taken a strong stand on the race question, I will criticize that church. And I feel that I am against that part of the religious system, because it was this system really, David, that I think brought about the communist revolution of 1918 in the Soviet Union.

Because the religious system had gotten tied into the political system and they were both corrupt, people wanted a change. Now, they didn't want to change as much as perhaps they got, but there was this terrific system that had become corrupt by 1917 and 1918 in the Soviet Union. I think that one of the things we must make a distinction [about] is there was a difference between the religious system and the political system. Jesus never did say anything against the political system, even though it was corrupt. He seemed to think this was outside His jurisdiction.[15]

Endnotes

1. "The David Frost Show," Westinghouse Broadcasting, 1970.

2. "Billy Graham: Churches Should Shun Partisan Politics." *U.S. News & World Report*, October 8, 1984, 12.

3. "A Prophet with Honor: David Frost documentary on Billy Graham," Channel Four, Great Britain, 1989.

4. Aikman, David. "Preachers, Politics and Temptation." *Time*, May 28, 1990, 12.

5. "The David Frost Show," Westinghouse Broadcasting, 1969.

6. "Watergate." *Christianity Today*, January 4, 1974, 9.

7. "A Prophet with Honor: David Frost documentary on Billy Graham," Channel Four, Great Britian, 1989.

8. *Ibid.*

9. *Ibid.*

10. Martin, William. *A Prophet with Honor: The Billy Graham Story*. (New York: William Morrow, 1991), 344.

11. "A Prophet with Honor: David Frost documentary on Billy Graham," Channel Four, Great Britain, 1989.

12. Martin, William. *A Prophet with Honour: The Billy Graham Story*. (New York: William Morrow, 1991), 359.

13. "A Prophet with Honour: David Frost documentary on Billy Graham," Channel Four, Great Britain, 1989.

14. "Reverend Billy Graham Talking with David Frost," PBS, January 29, 1993.

15. "The David Frost Show," Westinghouse Broadcasting, 1970.

CHAPTER 4

Billy Graham
on
Preaching, Evangelism, and the Bible

You have a voice that pulls. God can use that voice of yours. He can use it mightily.

College President Bob Jones
trying to convince student
Billy Graham to stay at his school.

Billy once described himself as "a simple country preacher who preaches a simple gospel."[1] Yet this simple country preacher has preached to some 210 million people in 185 countries. He says only God knows how many people he's brought to Christ: "I think God brings them and I'm just an instrument in His hands."[2]

I first interviewed Billy for the London *Daily Mail* newspaper during his 1963 crusade in Paris. No one I asked in Paris had seemed to know quite where the meetings were being held, though, to be fair, this was not so much a reflection on Billy's crusade as on my French. . . . When the service began, the hymns were sung in French, but the "sacred solos" by George Beverly Shea were in English, preceded by a translation. As Mr. Shea's first song was "He's Got the Whole World in His Hands" the interpreter's main task was to repeat the words *dans ses mains, dans ses mains* approximately twenty-seven times.

Eventually, after all the preliminaries, came the message. I was fascinated to discover that Billy's impact was in no way diminished by having to speak through an interpreter.

During that interview in Paris, Billy talked about his experiences in London. "I was frightened. That's why I left England in 1954," he said. "I don't want people pointing at me. I just want to point them to Jesus. And in 1954 I got frightened. I began to feel it was Billy Graham people were interested in, not Jesus Christ. I went to see the Archbishop of Canterbury—he was a good friend—and said that I could go anywhere in England and fill any stadium, but that I was worried.

"I explained why, and said that perhaps I should leave England. The Archbishop said that he thought that might be a good idea. But perhaps I was wrong. Perhaps if I'd gone all over England, there could have been a great revival. . . . If I had known the right way to do it. . . ."

In the *Daily Mail* I fell to wondering what might have happened. Would we have become a nation as dull and narrow-minded as some of his followers? Or a nation as vibrantly alive and flagrantly Christian as Dr. Graham himself? I wish he'd stayed.

Thinking about the way he preached in 1954, when I first heard him, and his preaching in the 1960s, I noticed differences. I talked to him about this during our first television interview.

> **Frost:** Isn't it true to say—I'm just thinking of hearing you in Paris last year and hearing you at Harringay, what, ten years ago, and there seemed to me in your own message not to be a new message . . . but certainly to be a new emphasis. Your own message in the last ten years has altered, matured, done something, hasn't it?
>
> **Graham:** I'm not sure that the basic message has changed, but I would say it's expressed, perhaps, in different terms here and there. I stress a great deal the love of God from the cross saying to the whole world, "I love you, I love you, I will forgive you," and the need of man's response.
>
> I think perhaps that is an emphasis that was not as strong ten years ago in my preaching as it is today because I do

believe that man is held accountable to God and is going to stand at the judgment. He needs to repent of sin, he needs to turn to Christ, but there's the love element, I think, that's most important in the Gospel.

Frost: And why has it changed in ten years though? Why is there now more emphasis—I think there is—on the love of God in what you do and less on the effects if you ignore the love of God? This is a change.

Graham: Well, first of all, I was not trained theologically in a theological college. I picked up my theology as I went along because my work, before I came into evangelistic preaching, was in education. And I think I've been studying and growing and perhaps, I hope at least, have a fuller understanding of what the Gospel really is, that it is good news to a man that is lost and confused and frustrated about purpose and meaning in life.[3]

"Do you have good nights and bad nights when you are preaching?" I asked. "And how do you evaluate your efforts?"

Frost: If one is doing something confessedly earthly like writing an article or something and one decides afterwards that there's a sentence that would have been much better if you hadn't been off form and put it rather badly, well, there's a great feeling of chagrin or whatever you wanted to call it.

Now, if . . . you're at a meeting and 200 or 250 people may make this most vital step of their lives, what is the feeling . . . afterwards . . . that you were off form? Because in a sense, in your terms, this is much more important because perhaps 200 people rather than 250 have come forward.

Graham: I believe that when the Gospel is preached, however badly and however many mistakes it may be, and the average clergyman, myself or anyone, [is speaking], that the Holy Spirit is the communicating agent; that people are really not listening to me after about ten or fifteen minutes if I'm really preaching the Gospel. I think they're listening to another voice inside, the voice of the Holy Spirit, and the Holy Spirit is applying and communicating. That's the reason I disagree with the Bishop of Woolwich in that we need a new jargon to appeal to this generation. We don't at all. We need the old jargon, the biblical jargon, preached in the power and urgency of the Holy Spirit. And I believe the Holy Spirit is the communicating agent because there's something inside the human heart, when truth is preached, that says, "Yes, that's it."

Now, I know that I may preach it rather poorly and I know that maybe some evening I may not be feeling up to par physically and all the rest of it and I may leave out many things that I wanted to say. But God knows my motive and He knows my heart and God uses even that simple presentation that might have been poorly done and He applies it to the human heart because salvation, the Bible says, is of God.

Frost: So in that sense, there can never be a feeling that "I've done badly, I've failed tonight"?

Graham: Oh, I have that feeling quite often. In fact, most of the time, I feel I wish I could have represented the Gospel better tonight. Really, that's a sincere feeling. Almost every night I say, "I wish I had done much better," because I'm a representative, really, of Christ there. I'm saying, "Be ye reconciled to God in the name of Jesus Christ," and that's a tremendous responsibility.[4]

I recall a story about Billy's first preaching experience in a small North Carolina jail. After evangelist Jimmie Johnson preached to the inmates, he unexpectedly called on Billy to tell of his conversion. After beginning with the inappropriate greeting, "I'm so glad to see so many of you out this afternoon," the scared young Billy gave his testimony. The experience convinced him once again that he never would become a preacher.[5] With this background, I wondered when he knew he had been called to preach the Gospel.

> **Graham:** I don't think that ever came at a moment. I think it gradually evolved. My first series of evangelistic meetings took place in 1938, which was very early after my call to Christian service, and I had prepared four sermons. I remember the first time I ever preached in a church. I had [the sermons] ready and I thought each one would last forty-five minutes, and I stood up in this small congregation of about thirty-five people and I preached all four of them in eight minutes.
>
> I'm still nervous when I stand up to preach. I always get tense and nervous and afraid that I may say something that would mislead people. You know, it's a tremendous responsibility to try to tell people how to get to heaven.[6]

We talked about the beginnings of the crusades in Los Angeles in 1949, before Billy was well known.

> **Frost:** The Billy Graham show was on the road to win souls for Christ.
>
> **Graham:** We hadn't but a few lines in the press. I had been taken by the committee to see the mayor of the city of

Los Angeles, and they had a line about that in the *Los Angeles Times*, but nothing else.

Frost: Nothing, that is, until the newspaper baron William Randolph Hearst, great propagator of anticommunist rhetoric, spied Graham's potential and put out the order, "Puff Graham."

Graham: He and Marion Davies put on some old clothes and camouflaged themselves and sat in that tent and listened, and as a result of that, he put out this statement that said, "Puff Graham."

So one night I went and I saw several photographers and there were several reporters trying to interview me all at one time, and I said, "What has happened? Why are you here?" They said, "You've just been kissed by William Randolph Hearst."[7]

Hearst's embrace gave Billy the power to realize a driving ambition to conquer the United States for Christ. I discovered an insightful article he wrote about the impact of that Los Angeles crusade on his preaching. He said, "I found my sermons and statements being analyzed and criticized by hundreds of clergy, laymen, and theologians throughout the world. . . . To say the least, I was baffled . . . and even frightened. Over and over again I went to my knees for guidance and direction."[8]

Billy described his preaching style to me, which he's maintained throughout his ministry:

Graham: I decided that I would just adopt that style of hitting hard and starting with issues right out of the newspaper, right off the ticker tape that day, and catch people's ear. Sometimes people would tell me, "You know, we learned about events from you, by listening to you."[9]

As God's ambassador, Billy Graham has privileged access across the globe. He told me how his world role began in Britain in 1954.

Graham: When I got off the train at Waterloo Station, it was jammed with thousands of people, and somebody here had raised the question in one of the papers which had been carried to the House of Commons and they made speeches as to whether this strange person from America that's called an evangelist was going to come over here and disrupt things.

The British have a marvelous way, that if you're sort of beaten down and they feel that you're being unfairly so, they flock to you, and that began to happen and it began to happen in the press as well. The press turned around, so that within three or four weeks, the press was largely on our side and they were carrying huge stories and people were coming from everywhere to attend it. . . .

When we finished after three months here . . . we had invitations to every major European country and we took them and we toured Europe.

(As an interesting footnote to his European tour, I learned that the stadium in Berlin where Hitler had used his unholy rhetoric to such effect was where Billy Graham shouted his hopes for peace over the Iron Curtain.)[10]

"What does the responsibility for the crusades take out of you?" I wondered. The preparation, as well as delivering the sermons each night, must be extremely demanding. I found one comment he made after the 1957 New York crusade most revealing.

"I have notes in front of me. I have prepared each one of my sermons. My greatest chore in New York, in a sense, was preparing a new address every night, and so I should say I averaged about four or five hours of study every day while I was there in preparation for these talks. In most cases I had notes. Sometimes they were very extensive notes; sometimes they were just two or three words on a scrap of paper. . . . I never memorize. I don't do any memorization except the Scriptures."[11]

He told me about two crusades that were particularly draining:

Graham: There were two crusades that took something out of me that probably will never be replaced physically, and one was the London crusade ten years ago [1954] here when I preached every night at Harringay Arena for three months. Now, when I left, I was twenty-two pounds less weight and a nervous energy went out of me. And then in the New York crusade, I preached sixteen weeks at Madison Square Garden without a break and something went out of me there.

If I had it to do over again, I don't think I would stay so long. Our crusades [now] are much shorter.[12]

Billy Graham told me that he helped pay for his education by delivering milk and selling Fuller brushes door-to-door. He apparently did well as a salesman, and I wanted to know if the experience made him a better public speaker.

Graham: Oh, I would think so, because I was naturally sort of a shy fellow, and I didn't particularly like to meet people, and that got me over that. And I think it allowed me to talk with people and to sell people. I never took a speech course in my life. I never have read a book on speech. Because the way I speak in the pulpit is my natural form of speaking.[13]

In 1969, we talked about the crusade recently held in New York City, including the impact of television on the crusade.

Frost: I was delighted to read that the crusade recently at Madison Square Garden went so well.

Graham: It was a bit of a surprise to us, because we had it on television three times a day in New York and at night at primetime and we had it throughout the Eastern seaboard. And we thought that being live on television, or delayed an hour or two, would cut our audiences down, but it seemed to work the other way, and I was quite surprised, because the Garden was jammed to capacity and overflowing every night except one, when they had a rainstorm. But it was really a tremendous reception, so overwhelming that there's a great deal of talk about the possibility of coming back next year to the Garden and keeping our organization very much intact as we did in London.[14]

At the end of the 1989 London crusade—or mission, the term Billy was trying to use—we had this conversation:

Frost: The mission now has a triumphant conclusion. There's more than a million people you've spoken to, haven't you?

Graham: Yes. I think about a million and a quarter people have been in the meetings themselves, and then we reached other people by satellite television throughout Africa and other parts of the world.

Frost: Now, what about last night, that storm? I mean, the pictures on the news of you with your raincoat on and the pelting-down rain. When you saw the pelting-down rain, did you feel like saying, "God, why are you doing this to me?"

Graham: I was at Wembley in 1955 every night for a week, and it rained every single night except one. Then it turned ice cold. And the people all stayed. There's some quality within the British people that gives them that staying power that's a strength in British society. And they didn't leave. Nobody left, as far as I know, and they were as quiet and as still, and when I gave the appeal to receive Christ, more than 4,000 responded out on that muddy field.

Frost: And walking out into the rain?

Graham: That's right, into the rain.

Frost: Which they might have been sheltered before, but when they made their decision, they knew— .

Graham: They came right out. And it pretty well ceased raining, it was just drizzling when they came forward, but we had a downpour and the lightening hit the stadium, and I think everybody thought God was speaking from Mount Sinai ready to give another Ten Commandments.

Frost: Thou shalt not . . . What are your conclusions about the British at this moment in time?

Graham: I think that there's a great hunger in this country for the simple, authoritative proclamation of the Gospel of Jesus Christ, and I think that some people feel that they're not getting it in all their churches. And the churches where they are preaching simple Gospel messages, very much like George Whitefield or John Wesley preached, the churches are packed out.[15]

We all know how much Billy quotes the Bible throughout his sermons, and I asked which verse meant the most to him.

Graham: Well, the one that I've preached on the most

is John 3:16, and it's the best-known verse.

Frost: "For God so loved . . ."

Graham: "For God so loved the world, that He gave His only begotten Son, that whosoever believeth in him should not perish, but have everlasting life." Now, the thing that gets me in that verse is when He says, "whosoever." That means the whole world. Whatever color a person's skin, whatever language he speaks, God loves him. And God is willing to save him. And that to me is marvelous. There are twenty-five words in the English translation of that.[16]

Even the great preachers of the world won't reach everyone. Billy was once asked how he felt about someone who isn't interested in the Gospel. He said, "I just want to shake them and say, oh, if you only knew Jesus Christ. If He lived in your heart, you could have a peace about [your problems]."[17] I also wondered what he thinks about people who *are* interested.

Frost: As you see people coming forward in your campaigns . . . to make their decision, what do you think as you see hundreds of people coming forward? What thoughts are going through your mind?

Graham: The parable of the sower, in which Jesus indicated that there were four types of soil that the Word of God lands upon. And a fourth of those are, will go on to grow in the grace and knowledge of Christ and become true disciples, but three-fourths of those will not. For various reasons, they'll drop out. Maybe the pressure and the allurements of the world, or maybe the materialism, or whatever it may be will wipe all that out. And Jesus spelled that out very carefully in the Gospels. And I don't know that one could say that a fourth—He didn't say a fourth—but He had four different categories, and I've always thought that in any group that comes forward to make a commitment, if I've preached the Gospel faithfully, a fourth of them will be there five years from now or ten years from now.[18]

Billy Graham is certainly a preacher among preachers. He once said, "I am a proclaimer of the message of the Bible. I am not preaching some new idea, some new philosophy, or something I have thought up. I am simply preaching the Bible, the same old truths that the church has believed for centuries.[19]

"But what is the gift that you have that other preachers don't?" I asked.

> **Graham:** I think, David, that God gave me the gift of an evangelist. The Bible teaches that there's the gift of the pastor, there's a gift of a teacher, and there's a gift of an evangelist. Now, the church, through the years, in my judgment, has neglected the gift of the evangelist. And yet that is a gift that God gives to certain people.[20]

One of the first times we met, I wanted to know how Billy Graham interpreted the Bible. "Are you a Bible literalist? And what about evolution versus creationism?"

> **Graham:** I don't think anyone is really a literalist because you don't say that, when Jesus gave the parable of the rich man that had died and gone to hell and the poor man that had gone to heaven—He said that he went to Abraham's

bosom. Now, that didn't mean that he literally climbed down into Abraham's bosom. So no one really is a complete literalist in the Bible. We know when we read the Bible, our common sense tells us.

Frost: But, I mean, what do you view—do you view, for instance, the creation of the world as it's shown in the Bible as a parable and, at the same time, accept scientific suggestions about the age of the world?

Graham: Oh, I don't think that there's any conflict at all between science today and the Scriptures. I think that we have misinterpreted the Scriptures many times and we've tried to make the Scriptures say things that they weren't meant to say, and I think we have made a mistake by thinking that the Bible is a scientific book.

The Bible is not a book of science. The Bible is a book of redemption, and of course, I accept the Creation story. I believe that God did create the universe. I believe He created man, and whether it came by an evolutionary process and at a certain point He took this person or this being and made him a living soul or not, does not change the fact that God did create man.

Frost: But the fact remains, doesn't it, Mr. Graham, that what you're saying you are, in fact, in one way or another modifying the Bible a bit and looking at it through your own understanding? Now, if you modify that story or one or two or the others that you've mentioned, how do you decide where you stop modifying—

Graham: I didn't modify because I didn't finish. I personally believe that it's just as easy to accept the fact that God took some dust and blew on it and out came a man as it is to accept the fact that God breathed upon man and he became a living soul and it started with some protoplasm and went right on up through the evolutionary process. Either way is by faith and whichever way God did it makes no difference as to what man is and man's relationship to God.

Frost: I'm sure you also sort of modify the various statements that always rolled out about—in the Old Testament about that adulterers should be stoned—

Graham: Oh, no, no, no, no, because you see God—this was the law of Israel and this is not our law today and Christ changed all that when He came. But I don't modify that at all because that actually happened. That was the law of Israel. . . .

It's not for today, though, because you see, God dealt with people in different methods. For example, in the Old Testament, they were under law and in the New Testament we're under grace. And when Jesus Christ came, He was the fulfillment of all the law and He said the fulfillment of the law is love.[21]

Billy has said, "If ever there was a woman called to God to proclaim the Scriptures, my daughter Anne is the one. She's one of the great Bible teachers among women today. I have a great appreciation for her and other women who have a gift of God." I recently asked him, "Does that mean that you are in favor of the ordination of women?"

Graham: It would be according to the circle I was in, because I feel that I belong to all the churches. I am equally at home in an Anglican or Baptist church or a Brethren assembly or a Roman Catholic church, and I would have to say that I would identify with the customs and the culture and the theology of that particular church.

Frost: But do you welcome that development?

Graham: Yes. Women preach all over the world as for-eign missionaries, and it doesn't offend—it doesn't bother me at all from my study of the Scriptures, and there were many women preachers in the Bible.[22]

As Billy Graham's ministry has expanded, he has often been asked to interpret the church's role. Even in the early days of his ministry he was concerned that churchgoing wasn't related to people's daily lives.[23]

I wondered why religion doesn't focus on developing our potentialities, making life fuller and richer, instead of narrower—as outsiders usually see it.

Graham: I think that we have really, the church, all of us, and I'm included, have probably sometimes given a caricature of Christianity. You see, Christianity was not something just in the four walls of the cathedral in the first century. It was called "the Way." It was a way of life that dominated my entire life, and it was a dynamic that pushed these early Christians throughout the entire world until they turned the world upside down.

And they were not professionals. These people had no Bibles. They had no theological colleges. They had none of the modern things that we have today, and yet they turned their world upside down, a pagan world. Now, what did they have? They had a dynamic. They had a life. They had an experience with the living Christ, and I think the great problem in the church in Britain and America and throughout the world is that we have failed to impress upon people that it is a living experience every day with Jesus Christ.[24]

Do you enjoy going to church? I inquired.

Frost: I know a great many preachers, in fact, feel odd going to a church where someone else is conducting services. Do you?

Graham: No, I love it.

Frost: You like other people's services?

Graham: Oh, yes, I do. I listen on the radio in America every Sunday almost all day long to other preachers, and then I go to church and I love to hear preaching. I love the liturgy of the church; I love the worship of the church.

Frost: When you go to a service, what's the most important part of it for you?

Graham: To me, the most important part, of course, is the Communion service, when I have the opportunity to fellowship at the Lord's Table and take of this wine that is representative of His blood and of the bread that represents His body.

Frost: In those cases where you go to church, in fact, that's more important than the message?

Graham: To me it is, in that sense. And then the message, of course, is important in this sense because we've gotten away, I think more so in Britain than America, in the emphasis on preaching. I would like to see a return back to emphasis on preaching, because the Bible says God has chosen the foolishness of preaching to save those that believe.[25]

Billy was once quoted as saying, "I believe in the Devil and I believe in God and I'm trying to get people to vote for God."[26] And just a few years ago he said he thought there was more sin in the world now than when he began his ministry—because there are more people.[27] In a reflective moment, I looked back at Billy Graham's ministry, from the 1940s until today and asked, "Who's winning? God or the Devil?"

> **Graham:** Ultimately, God is going to win. At the moment, it seems the Devil is winning. I think that there seems to be more wickedness, more crime, more drugs, more disregard of God than ever before. But at the same time, something else is happening. Who would have ever dreamed a few years ago that Eastern Europe would be opened up? Or that Russia would be pleading for Bibles and evangelists and preachers? And that you could go to any school in Russia and open the Bible and talk about Christ? And that they are wanting teachers to come and teach the Bible in the schools in the Soviet Union, when they're banned in this country by law? You can't talk about Christ. You can't even have Christmas carols in schools in this country, if you can imagine such a thing.[28]

Will Billy ever step down from the pulpit? He says, "I will never retire from preaching. I do not see anybody in the Bible who retires from preaching."[29]

More recently, however, he's modified that stance by saying he plans to continue preaching past the age of 80, or until he can no longer physically do the job.[30] As of now, he says, "When I go to the pulpit to preach, I may need a little help getting there. But when I get there I can sense the presence of the power of the Lord, and He helps me in my preaching."[31]

Endnotes

1. Cal Thomas on CNBC, May 5, 1996.
2. *Larry King Live*, Interview with Billy Graham, January 21, 1997.
3. "Doubts and Certainties: David Frost interview with Billy Graham," BBC-2, 1964.
4. *Ibid.*
5. Martin, William. *A Prophet with Honor: the Billy Graham Story* (New York: William Morrow, 1991) 68.
6. "A Prophet With Honor: David Frost documentary on Billy Graham," Channel Four, Great Britain, 1989.
7. *Ibid.*
8. Graham, Billy. "Ten Years Have Taught Me." *Christian Century*, February 17, 1960.
9. "A Prophet With Honor: David Frost documentary on Billy Graham," Channel Four, Great Britain, 1989.
10. *Ibid.*
11. "Does a Religious Crusade Do Any Good? Interview with Billy Graham." *U.S. News & World Report*, September 1957.
12. "Doubts and Certainties: David Frost interview with Billy Graham," BBC-2, 1964.
13. *Ibid.*
14. "The David Frost Show," Westinghouse Broadcasting, 1969.
15. "Frost on Sunday: Interview with Billy Graham," TV-am, Great Britain, 1989.
16. "Reverend Billy Graham talking with David Frost," PBS, January 23, 1993.
17. *Donahue*, Interview with Billy Graham, October 11, 1979.
18. "Reverend Billy Graham talking with David Frost," PBS, January 23, 1993.
19. "Press Conference." *Decision Magazine*, September 1962, 14.
20. "The David Frost Show," Westinghouse Broadcasting, 1969.
21. "Doubts and Certainties: David Frost interview with Billy Graham," BBC-2, 1964.
22. "Reverend Billy Graham talking with David Frost," PBS, May 30, 1997.
23. *Meet the Press*, Interview with Billy Graham, June 9, 1957.
24. "Doubts and Certainties: David Frost interview with Billy Graham," BBC-2, 1964.
25. *Ibid.*
26. DuQuesne, Preston. "I Believe in the Devil but I Believe in God, Too." *National Tattler*, Spring 1974.
27. Aikman, David. "Preachers, Politics, and Temptation." *Time*, May 28, 1990, 12.
28. "Reverend Billy Graham talking with David Frost," PBS, January 23, 1993.
29. Aikman, David. "Preachers, Politics, and Temptation." *Time*, May 28, 1990, 12.
30. *Larry King Live*, Interview with Billy Graham, January 21, 1997.
31. Gilbreath, Edward. "The Lord's Crusader." *New Man Magazine*, April 1997, 28.

CHAPTER 5

Billy Graham
on
Pain and Suffering

For now we see through a glass darkly . . . but then I shall know even as also I am known.

The Apostle Paul
1 Corinthians 13:12

To his credit Billy doesn't offer pat spiritual answers to inexplicable things. Invariably, when disaster strikes, he is asked if he thinks God had a hand in it. Random floods, hurricanes, tornadoes—the sites of which he has often visited, offering comfort to the afflicted—beg the question, "Why?" But sometimes our problems are man-made, even more perplexing than so-called natural disasters.

A case in point was the 1995 Oklahoma City bombing. At the memorial service, at which President Clinton and Oklahoma Governor Keating also spoke, it was Billy Graham, I think, who offered the most comfort to those who had lost loved ones. He said, "At times like this, we'll do one of two things: They will either make us hard and bitter and angry at God, or they will make us tender and open and help us to reach out in trust and faith. . . . I pray that you will not let bitterness and poison creep into your souls, but you will turn in faith and trust in God even if we cannot understand. It is better to face something like this with God than without Him."[1]

When I asked him the age-old question, "Why does God allow pain and suffering?" Billy had a candid reply.

Frost: You've been battling Parkinson's disease for three years or so. Now, is God responsible for that?

Graham: I don't know. He allows it. And He allows it for a purpose that I may not know. I think everything that comes to our lives, if we are true believers, God has a purpose and a plan. And many of these things are things that cause suffering or inconvenience or whatever. But it helps to mature me because God is molding and making me in the image of His Son, Jesus Christ. Jesus Christ suffered more than any man that ever lived, because when He was on that cross, He was bearing the sins that you and I have committed. He was guilty of adultery. He was guilty of murder. He was guilty of everything you can think of. And He was guilty of our sins. Now, He suffered in a way that we could never understand.

Frost: But, I mean, for instance, I thank God for having three healthy sons.

Graham: Yeah.

Frost: But, maybe that's not logical really because if I am thanking God for three healthy sons, should the parents of a Down's syndrome baby be blaming God?

Graham: No. I don't think they should ever blame God. I think that God has allowed these things to happen in families through the years. And, a lady told me yesterday of all the troubles and difficulties in their family. She was from Colombia in South America, and she said, "I thank God for every bit of suffering I've had to go through because it's made me a woman of God and a strong woman. And I'm a better wife and a better mother as a result of the suffering I've had to go through."

Frost: You can't really say that though to the parents of a deformed child, can you? How should they look at it?

Graham: You've asked me a question that would be very difficult for me, because I think that there are some of these things that we'll never understand till we get to heaven. And I don't try to explain them because I don't know the explanation. I don't know why. I only know the general principle is that God is a God of love and mercy. And God is working in your life to make you conform to the image of His Son and suffering is part of life. We're told that we are going to suffer. Job said, "Man suffers as the sparks fly upward." And I think that we are suffering constantly, and we are going to suffer all of our lives.

Frost: But if you don't blame God for ill health, you can't thank Him for good health, can you?

Graham: I do. Everyday that I get up and feel good, I say, "Thank You, Lord" because I have . . . One day I feel good, the next day I feel badly, but I have to control that. That has to be controlled. In other words, I'm not going to say that every day should be good, or I wouldn't know what the bad is. Or every day bad, I wouldn't know what the good is. I think God allows us wonderful days and wonderful years and wonderful months, but then come tragedies. And as you get older, you find that you have problems—physical problems, maybe intellectual problems, marital problems, problems in your business. All these things come, many times, with old age.

Frost: But there are those things, as you were saying, like what do you say to the parents of a Down's syndrome child where in the end, you were saying, "I don't have all the answers"?

Graham: I don't have all the answers. I just know that I trust God, Who is a God of mercy. But I do not know why and I cannot explain to mothers who I have had to talk to and have had the privilege of talking to who have had a son wounded or had a son whose legs have been cut off in war or in a motor car accident, all of these things.[2]

I still find Billy's formulation difficult to take on board, but the fact that Billy Graham, once so roundly criticized as the apostle of an impossible certitude, could admit that there were questions to which he did not have an answer I found oddly reassuring: maybe the rest of us didn't need to feel so threatened by our doubts either.

And, according to Billy Graham, Christians aren't "exempt from the tribulations and natural disasters that come upon the world. Scripture does teach that the Christian can face tribulation, crisis, calamity, and personal suffering with a supernatural power that is not available to the person outside of Christ."[3] When we talked about pain and suffering again, Billy elaborated.

> **Frost:** Talking of God's plan, whenever we discuss religion, there's one subject in letters that always comes up. People write and say, for instance, they thank God for the birth of healthy children, but are they right to give God the credit for that because then doesn't He take the blame for children who are malformed?
>
> **Graham:** I would think that that's a question, David, that I cannot answer. I've been asked that question many times and I have written a book on the subject, but I still do not know the precise answers to why God allows some children to be born with deformities and other children to be born healthy. That's in God's hands, and the primary thing to keep in mind is, it's not the body that's so important in God's sight as it is the spirit or the soul of man. And Jesus said, "What shall it profit a man if he gain the whole world and loses his own soul?" So the soul and the spirit is the most important, and many people overlook that.
>
> **Frost:** But in that situation, should one say thank

You to God for the healthy children, or not? Or is that something that He doesn't get involved in because the world has rejected God?

Graham: No. I think He does get involved. I think He's involved in all of our lives because the Bible says He has the hairs of our head numbered and He loves us and He knows what is best for us. And it would be a horrible thing to think that God gives an unhealthy child to a person and that is best for them, but maybe in the long eternal look at it, it may be best. Maybe that child was used, as in the case of Roy Rogers. He and Dale Evans had a child that was malformed and they felt that the child absolutely saved their marriage and brought them much closer to God. And so, she wrote an article or a book entitled *Angel Unaware*. In other words, this little child became an angel to them.

Frost: It's terribly difficult for people to come to terms with that, though, isn't it?

Graham: Very difficult, and I don't have the answer. All I can do is comfort them and try to sympathize with them and suffer with them because that's what compassion means, that you enter into suffering with people.[4]

This reminds me of another interview Billy did in which he was asked about the tragedy of losing a young child. What do you say to the parents? he was asked. In his usual, straightforward style he answered: "I just tell them that God loves them, that there's a reason for it, and just accept the fact that God is a God of love, and He's not going to let anything happen to you or to that child unless there was a reason for it."[5]

When asked, "How do you suggest that Christians get ready for the hard times ahead?" Billy's answer was classic Billy Graham: "The most important thing we can do is grow in our relationship to Christ. If we have not learned to pray in our everyday lives, we will find it difficult to know God's peace and strength through prayer when the hard times come. If we have not learned to trust God's Word when times are easy, we will not trust His Word when we face difficulties. And I am convinced that one of the greatest things we can do is to memorize Scripture. The Scriptures speak to us in those moments when we look to the Lord for sustenance and strength."[6]

Of course, on the heels of questions about pain and suffering are questions about good and evil. Do you believe there is such a thing as evil, such a thing as the Devil? I inquired.

Graham: Yes. I definitely do. I think the Bible teaches there is a personality called the Devil, and I think there are millions of demons, and I think their power is growing in the world, because as we approach the end of history, not the end of the world, not the end of the human race, but the end of this historical period that we call the Age of the Spirit of God, I believe that Satan's activities are going to intensify in violence, in war, and all the disturbances that we now see taking place in the world. And I—yes, to answer your question directly, there is a Devil.

Frost: What's he like?

Graham: Well, the Bible tells us quite a bit about him. He's called the prince of the air—prince of this world. He's called the prince and power of the air. He's called the god of this age. He's said to have tremendous power. He doesn't have a body like yours or mine. We can't see him. He's not a fellow with horns and a red suit racing up and down the aisle.

Frost: He isn't?

Graham: You remember the old story, I'm sure—I think it happened here in England when a fellow dressed up in a red suit and he had horns and he had a pitchfork and he came into a church service on a Sunday morning in this little country church, and everybody flew out the windows and out the door. They were frightened. And this one lady sat on the front row, and she just kept sitting there. He went up with his pitchfork and said, "Aren't you afraid of me?" "Oh," she said, "no sir, Mr. Devil. I've been on your side all the time."

But, you see, he's not like that. The Bible says that he's a tremendous power that led a revolt against God. And apparently when he was banished from heaven in some mysterious way that I couldn't possibly explain, he landed on this planet. And this planet became a planet in rebellion. This is the one planet that God is most concerned about, insofar as we know. This is the planet that He was willing to send His Son to rescue us from the power of the Devil. And that's what the Gospel of Christ is all about. And the good news is, God says, "I'll restore you and forgive you and give you strength and power to face life and death."[7]

Billy Graham does not usually do movie reviews, but I recall his warning after seeing previews of *The Exorcist* and reading reviews of it. He said "Anyone who exposes himself to the Devil, even in a movie, is exposing himself to real danger. . . . I have heard some speculation that this film will bring people back to the church or renew faith in the ability of good to overcome evil and other

so-called benefits to be derived from it. But I hold no such hopes."[8]
If the Devil is a danger to other people, is he also a danger to Billy
Graham?

"Do you believe the Devil works on you?" I asked.

Graham: Yes, definitely. In fact, David, I think people
would be rather surprised. I sense it every day, because I'm
tempted every day and temptation comes from the Devil.
The Bible says God doesn't tempt any man. God will try a
person. He will test a person, but He doesn't tempt us to evil.
That's done by the Devil. And the Devil is constantly after a
person like me.

I was in France about three weeks ago, and the American
ambassador entertained us at a little dinner party. There was
a very famous French novelist there, and she came up to
me and spoke to me quite interestingly. She said, "Mr.
Graham, you know, I'm sure that you are the object of
tremendous evil forces. They want to attack you because you
are a provocation to evil."

I said, "Yes, I have sensed that. I have to be very careful
in the life I lead, in keeping up my defenses in prayer and
Bible study." Because the Bible says we're not up against flesh
and blood. We're up against principalities and powers and
forces of wickedness. We're up against a great spiritual force.
When anybody tries to stand out for the Gospel or stand out
for good, he's going to be opposed by these evil forces in the
world.[9]

Speaking of the Devil, Billy once wondered aloud in one of our
conversations why God created Lucifer.

Graham: I'd like to know why God created Lucifer. I'd like to know why sin was allowed to have such a power in the world. I would like to know why we've had so many wars and fighting in the name of religion. Those are things that puzzle me. The wars that are going on right now are largely religious wars. I mean, at least religion is involved in them. Those are things that puzzle me, and I don't know the answer to them. And I would like to know, because I have a curious mind like the average person does. I would like to know why God created so many planets and stars by the millions and billions if nobody's living on them. What's the purpose of all that? Why did God do that? I think I have many things I would like to ask the Lord someday, and I think I'll have the answer someday because the Bible says, "We shall know as we are known." In other words, we will have full knowledge someday.[10]

When we see people suffering and starving in places like Ethiopia or Somalia, I noted, some people come to the conclusion that there can't be a God. Billy's response:

Graham: But there is an answer to that, too, because there is another power at work in the world, and that's the power of the Devil. Satan is trying to disrupt everything that God is doing in the world. God is a God of love and mercy. And God loves all those people in Ethiopia. He loves all the people in Somalia. I remember when I was in India once, and they had a big tidal wave that came in. And I happened to be preaching just south of that. And I called the president of India, President Ray, whom I had just been with. And I asked him if I could have a helicopter from the military to fly to that place and to see those people and just identify with them. And I went.

Here were these bodies of beautiful women that had been in these bushes that caught by the thorns and the beautiful saris, and here were the crying of the children that saw some of them still left. Here were people moaning and groaning—25,000 people killed in ten minutes. And, I thought to myself, "How could God allow this?" I've stood at the side of people who were dying in war, for example, in Vietnam or in Korea.

I was in both of those wars in the sense that I was there as a chaplain to the troops at Christmastime to speak to them. And I'd go to those field hospitals and I'd see them with their legs cut off or I would see them in the most horrible conditions and I couldn't help but say, "Why?" And in my most recent meetings in Moscow—we had all over the city—we just had the word, "Why?" Why God allows suffering? Why do these things take place if God is a God of love? Why does this happen? And the answer is that there is a disease which is called in the Bible "sin." And this brings about cataclysmic judgments upon man.

Frost: And is this figure, Satan, the Devil, is he similar to God? And in opposition to God? Or is he a differently structured force?

Graham: Well, there are two, there are two large, long passages in the Bible about the beginnings of Satan. One is in the twenty-eighth chapter of Ezekiel and one is in the fourteenth chapter of Isaiah, in which he is described as "Lucifer, son of the morning." He was created by God, and apparently, he was the most beautiful and the greatest of all the angelic beings. And pride entered his heart. We don't know how, of course. I mean, there's no way that I can explain that.

He decided that he wanted to be like God. He wanted to have the power that God had. So he led a rebellion against God in heaven eons ago. And as a result of that, God banished him from heaven, and he landed on this planet. And God allowed him to have this planet, or at least as a place to reside. And he not only lived on the planet, but when God created man in His image to live on this planet, Satan came along and tempted man and man broke God's laws, rebelled against God.

So man himself is in rebellion against God. And that's where all this comes from. Now that's hard to take in. It's hard to understand if you don't believe. But you read the Bible and it's full of the fact that God is going to judge man, because God holds man responsible for his own sins. . . . You can say no to the Devil, or you can say yes. And all of us at some time in our lives say yes to him. We yield to the temptation. But the Bible says, "There's no temptation taken you, but such as is common to man. And God is faithful, who will not allow you to be tempted above that which you are able to bear, but will, with the temptation, make a way to escape." Every temptation you have, there's a way out.[11]

Endnotes

1. "Remarks by President, Governor and Dr. Graham at Memorial Service." *New York Times*, April 24, 1995, B8.
2. "Reverend Billy Graham talking with David Frost," PBS, January 29, 1993.
3. *The Billy Graham Christian Workers Handbook* (Minneapolis: World Wide Publications, 1984), 223.
4. "Frost on Sunday: Interview with Billy Graham," TV-am, Great Britain, 1989.
5. *Larry King Live*, Interview with Billy Graham, January 21, 1997.
6. "Candid Conversation with the Evangelist." *Christianity Today*, July 17, 1981, 23.
7. "The David Frost Show," Westinghouse Broadcasting, 1970.
8. "Billy Graham Tells Why He's Afraid to See *The Exorcist*." *National Inquirer*, March 31, 1984, 3.
9. "The David Frost Show," Westinghouse Broadcasting, 1970.
10. "Reverend Billy Graham talking with David Frost," PBS, January 29, 1993.
11. *Ibid.*

CHAPTER 6

Billy Graham
on
Presidents

I hardly ever go to a place, as President, that Billy Graham has not been there before me preaching. And I feel like a poor substitute, because a lot of the time what I'm trying to do is get people to lay down the hatred of the heart and reach down into their spirit and treat people who are different from themselves with the same respect that all God's children are entitled to. . . . I thank Billy and Ruth Graham for the ministry of their lives.

President Bill Clinton
May 6, 1996

*N*o preacher in the history of this country has had so much access to so many presidents as Billy Graham. How did it happen? I asked. He explained how in this interview with me.

Graham: Politics has always sort of fascinated me. It intrigued me, and also I began to realize that I could have some influence on the country spiritually, and that was true.

Frost: [You] have been friendly with every United States President since Harry S. Truman, whether on the golf course or in the White House.

Graham: Every time I'm with some of these people, I never leave without trying to say a word about what Christ can do and what God can do in their lives.[1]

Frost: Your first encounter with the White House has slightly mixed memories for you, I guess. That was President Truman, wasn't it?

Graham: Right.

Frost: And how did that come about?

Graham: Well, I was called one day by a congressman who—and I've heard two versions of this—but I was called by this particular congressman, [John] McCormack, who later became Speaker of the House from Massachusetts. I'd just held meetings all across New England. He was very warm toward me. And the Roman Catholic—he was Roman Catholic—and the Roman Catholic cardinal there was very warm toward me. His name was [Richard] Cushing. He preached John Kennedy's funeral, if you remember. And he was sort of the father that the Kennedy family looked to. And he wrote me up in his diocesan paper one day, and said, "Bravo, Billy." And that was back in the days when Protestants and Catholics didn't have much to do with each other in this country.

So John McCormack called me one day and he said, "How would you like to meet President Truman?" I said, "I would love to meet him." I said, "I've never met a president before." He said, "Well, I think we can arrange it. Would you come to Washington if we got it arranged?" I said, "Of course, I would be honored to." So, I was in Indiana, and Cliff Barrows and two or three of us went to Washington. And it was arranged for me to see the president. We went in to see him, the three or four of us, and he told us that he lived by the Golden Rule and that he always had a Bible. And we talked about religious things. We didn't talk about political things. As we were leaving after about twenty or thirty minutes of conversation, I asked him, "Could we have prayer?" And he said, "Well, I guess it wouldn't do much harm." So I put my arm around him, 'cause he was a small man compared to me, and I think he was a little surprised at that. And I prayed. And as I was praying, Cliff Barrows was saying, "Amen, Lord. Bless him. Bless him."

And so we left. Nobody had briefed us. I did not know that you didn't quote the president or anybody like that. And I learned a great lesson that has helped me through the years—not to quote famous people. The press surrounded me and they said, "What did you say to the president?" I told them. They said, "Well, what did he say to you?" And I told them. And they said, "Well, did you have prayer with him?" We said, "Yes." They said, "We didn't get a picture of that, do you mind going out here on the White House lawn and kneeling down and let us get a picture of you in prayer."

And I said, "No, I'll be happy to." And I went out there, like a fool, of course, and did that. And that was on the front page of the papers all across America: PRESIDENT PRAYS WITH EVANGELIST.

Then I read in Drew Pearson's column a few weeks later that said, "Billy Graham is persona non grata at the White House." And I didn't pay any attention to that. But after Truman left the White House, I went to Independence, Missouri, to see him and apologized. I said, "I've learned a big lesson." He said, "Oh, my, I knew they hadn't briefed you. I understood the whole thing." He said, "Don't think about it." I went to see him several times at Independence. And we became very friendly to each other. As time went on, my admiration for Truman grew, and so that was how we got into the White House.[2]

Billy has said, "Of all the presidents, I knew Eisenhower best and saw him the most. Although Ike was a well-loved president, I took a lot of criticism because of my close relationship with him. That was in the fifties, when I almost identified Americanism with Christianity, which you can see for yourself if you read some of my early sermons."[3] I asked him about their relationship.

Graham: Yes. We had a very close relationship. In fact, one of the closest I've had with any president. It started through a friend in Texas by the name of Sid Richardson. He was a very wealthy oil man that I got acquainted with while I was preaching in Texas. I was about the only preacher he ever went to hear preach. He would not hear anybody else. But he somehow liked me. I don't know why . . . and he was

Eisenhower's great friend and he was Eisenhower's great backer trying to get Eisenhower to run for president. And so, he asked me if I would write a letter to Eisenhower as to why he should run for president. So, I wrote a letter, but I didn't say that he should run for president. Why any American that was that popular and that many people wanted him, why he should offer himself. And so, Eisenhower wrote back and he said that was the . . . he used a . . .

Frost: Expletive. Expletive.

Graham: Yes. He used a word that I don't use, let's say. In saying that was the greatest letter he'd read and said, "I'd like to meet that young man." Said, "I think he could give me a good perspective on the youth of America." So, Mr. Richardson paid our way to go to Paris where he was head of SHAPE [Supreme Headquarters of the Allied Powers in Europe]. And Ruth and I went out there, and he kept me for about three or four hours. And we talked about everything under the sun.

For some reason, he got it in his mind that I wrote speeches, so that when he became nominated for president in Chicago at the Blackstone Hotel, he invited me to come up there. And I went up there. And he said, "Now, I want you to help me in this campaign." And he said, "Would you come and help me write some of my speeches? I want to put something religious and spiritual in them." He said, "I think I was elected partially because the country is in need of spiritual renewal."

So, I went to Denver where he stayed after he had been nominated and he kept me at the hotel there with him. And I met with him several times and talked with him and gave him suggestions and ideas, and I gave him a red Bible, which he kept the rest of his life. It is referred to in a number of newspaper accounts, that he always kept that red Bible beside him. And I had marked it up and it had notes in it about how to study the Bible and special places in the Bible. And I had many religious talks with him. But our great interest, I suppose, became golf because we played many games of golf together. And he was one of the great men that I knew.[4]

Though Billy Graham says he tried to keep his relationships with presidents on a spiritual plane, political advice was asked of him, and he was not averse to giving his opinion. When did he begin giving them advice, I wondered.

Graham: The first president, I think, that really asked me in depth was Eisenhower when he was sending troops into Little Rock. He called me that morning. I was in New York preaching in Madison Square Garden, and he called and said he was thinking about sending troops down there to stop it. He said, "What do you think?" I said, "I don't think you have an alternative." I said, "This is a terrible thing."

Within an hour, Nixon called. He was vice president. I told him the same thing. They sent troops into Little Rock, I believe, the next day.[5]

And Billy Graham went to Little Rock to help defuse the hatred that existed there. I discovered that Bill Clinton recalled many years later the enormity of Billy's contribution. He said, "There were those who asked Billy Graham to segregate his audience [in Little Rock]. . . . And I'll never forget that he said—and it was in the paper—that if he had to speak the Word of God to a segregated audience, he would violate his ministry, and he would not do it. And at the most intense time in the modern history of my state, everybody caved, and blacks and whites together poured into the football stadium. And when the invitation was given, they poured down together, down the aisles, and they forgot that they were supposed to be mad at each other, angry at each other, that one was supposed to consider the other somehow less than equal.

"And he never preached a word about integrating the schools. He preached the Word of God. And he lived it by the power of his example."[6]

Next came President Kennedy whose election Billy Graham opposed, but whose friendship he won. Just before the inauguration, Kennedy invited Billy to Palm Beach to play golf—at the suggestion of Joseph Kennedy, John's father. One of my favorite anecdotes from that meeting is best told by Billy: "On the first tee, I didn't hit the ball very far. . . . And he said, 'I always understood that you were a good golfer.' And I said, 'Well, I am if I am not playing with the president-elect of the United States.'"[7]

Billy has said that Kennedy was the only president he didn't know before his election, and even when they became acquainted they didn't see each other frequently. Billy commented, "When your picture appears in the press two or three times a year with a president, especially if it's on the golf course, it looks as if you are old buddies. But I really did not get to know John Kennedy."[8] I asked about their friendship, both on and off the golf course.

Graham: I'd become quite an admirer of Kennedy because he'd invited me several times to the White House and he had also come to all of our prayer breakfasts that we had in Washington, of which I was the speaker each time, and I'd gotten to know him a little bit and had come to admire him.[9]

Kennedy was the first president to talk to Billy about Vietnam. In retrospect, Billy says, "I felt that we were on the verge of something we might not be able to get out of." Today he regrets not speaking out against it.[10]

Billy Graham's relationship with Richard Nixon has been well documented. He knew him as a congressman, knew his Quaker parents, knew him as a vice president. I've seen letters that Billy Graham sent to Richard Nixon following his 1960 defeat. In one of those letters, now part of the public record, Billy consoled his friend and made an accurate prophecy: "I am convinced that temporary loss is going to be for the purpose of developing you into a greater leader for the task and responsibilities that are going to be yours in the next few years. I am equally convinced that you will be the next president of the United States."[11]

I suggested that of his presidential friends Billy was probably closest to Johnson and Nixon. Of President Johnson Billy said, "We enjoyed each other's company, but we never talked politics. However, I did take a lot of criticism in those days because of my friendship with a president who was stepping up the war in Vietnam.[12]

"You almost stayed from the Johnson administration to the Nixon administration, didn't you?" I asked during Nixon's first term.

Graham: Yes, Mr. Johnson's last weekend, that weekend of the inauguration, my wife and I were his only house guests that weekend. We went to church with him on his last Sunday, and we stayed over. And on the Monday morning when Mr. Nixon was inaugurated, the next day, of course I was on the platform and gave the inaugural prayer. And a very sweet and wonderful little thing happened that I've never heard anybody mention. But when the inauguration ceremony was over, and I was sitting right behind Vice President Humphrey and President Johnson—Mr. Nixon was now the President of the United States. He and his family left first. And then as the Johnson family left, Linda came over to me and kissed me, and so did Luci—right on the platform—and walked on out with their father and mother. And it was rather sweet, I thought, because we were very good friends with the Johnsons, and I love the Johnsons very much as people. I think they're a marvelous family.

Frost: How would you compare Lyndon Johnson and Richard Nixon as men?

Graham: I think their philosophy is probably quite alike. They both have many things in common, but their technique and approach and method is just totally different. Mr. Johnson is a great activist and moves things very fast. Mr. Nixon is a great student. He studies and reads and thinks things through. . . . His actions are quite deliberate. And I think personally that Richard Nixon is the best-trained man that's ever been in the White House. I doubt if we've ever had a man in history that so prepared himself for the White House. But I think one of the problems he's running into, and any President is going to run into, is that some people think that America may have reached the point where it cannot be governed, that the problems are now so overwhelming.

And, as a matter of fact, I said this in my inaugural prayer, which *Time* magazine said that Billy Graham gave his own inauguration address in the prayer. But I did say in the prayer that the problems were almost insoluble, and they are. The Democratic Party tried for many years. The Republican Party is trying. The problems are there, and it doesn't seem to have solution. And I think that Mr. Nixon is right when he says that ours is a spiritual crisis and unless we have a renewal of the American spirit, which I believe is based upon a religious spirit, I don't think we can solve some of these problems. Look at the economic problem or the race problem or the crime problem or the revolutionary problem or the student problem. All of these are problems that are beyond the ability of a president to cope with.

And another thing that's been interesting to me in knowing these various men is how limited their power really is. We think of a president as being all powerful. Well, he can push that button in an international war. There's no doubt about that. In that sense, he is powerful. But when it comes to solving these great problems like student unrest and all that, he's extremely limited in power. He can lead, he can influence and all of that, but that's about as far as he can go.[13]

Billy has also talked about his relationship with President Nixon during and after Watergate. He says, "I feel that I didn't misjudge *him*, but that I misjudged what he would do under certain pressures. I think there came a point [during Watergate] when he cracked under all those pressures and was no longer the Nixon I had known and admired.[14] Billy adds that during the last six months of Nixon's presidency he could not reach him. Billy's since learned that Nixon gave orders to keep him away so that he would not be scarred by Watergate. But after Nixon left the White House, they resumed their friendship.[15]

In an interview during President Clinton's first term, Billy made a comment that may explain how he has gotten along with such diverse men. He said, when asked what he thought of Clinton, "I think of him as the president, who was elected by the people, and we ought to support him as far as we can. . . . It is important to support the president—to build a wall of prayer around him. . . . That doesn't mean that you don't have a right to ask him questions and go into it."[16]

A few years ago I had the opportunity to talk to him about President Clinton. "Do you know him, also?"

Graham: I can't recall exactly the moment I first met Bill Clinton, but I remember the first time I had a long in-depth conversation with him was in Boise, Idaho, in the Governor's Conference that I had addressed. And he asked to see me, and I saw him. And I've seen him, I've met him on a number of occasions as we have known each other. And I have read in the press, and he has said publicly on the platform in Little Rock that he had come to our meeting when he was thirteen years of age and had made a great change in his life. He also remarked about the change that came in Arkansas racially because of our meetings that we held in Arkansas in those days. And I've had conversations with him since, and with his wife, Hillary. I remember one two-hour conversation Hillary and I had together. And she is a brilliant woman. It's too early to tell, of course, which direction his administration is going to take. It's the people around the president that run the thing. There's only so many people he can get to know personally and have conversations with and get his ideas over.[17]

Endnotes

1. "A Prophet with Honor: David Frost documentary on Billy Graham," Channel Four, Great Britain, 1989.

2. "Reverend Billy Graham Talking with David Frost," PBS, January 29, 1993

3. Beam, James Michael. "I Can't Play God Anymore." *McCall's*, January 1978, 100.

4. "Reverend Billy Graham Talking with David Frost," PBS, January 29, 1993.

5. "A Prophet with Honor: David Frost documentary on Billy Graham," Channel Four, Great Britain, 1989.

6. Bill Clinton's "Remarks at a dinner honoring Billy and Ruth Graham," *The Weekly Compilation of Presidential Documents*, May 6, 1996.

7. *Larry King Live*, Interview with Billy Graham, January 21, 1997.

8. Beam, James Michael. "I Can't Play God Anymore." *McCall's*, January 1978, 100.

9. "A Prophet with Honor: David Frost documentary on Billy Graham," Channel Four, Great Britain, 1989.

10. *Larry King Live*, Interview with Billy Graham, January 21, 1997.

11. Letter from Richard Nixon to Billy Graham, National Archives, February 2, 1961.

12. Beam, James Michael. "I Can't Play God Anymore." *McCall's*, January, 1978, 100.

13. "A Conversation with Billy Graham." *The David Frost Show*, December 1970.

14. Beam, James Michael. "I Can't Play God Anymore." *McCall's*, January, 1978, 100.

15. Aikman, David. "Preachers, Politics and Temptation." *Time*, May 28, 1990, 12.

16. "Press Conference." *Decision Magazine*, September 1962, 14.

17. "Reverend Billy Graham Talking with David Frost," PBS, January 29, 1993.

CHAPTER 7

Billy Graham
on
Sin and Temptation

Billy Graham is not unlike Melville's Billy Budd with his 'raw childlike unblinking goodness, possessing a staggering passion for the pure, the sanitary, the wholesome, the upright.'

Marshall Frady
Billy Graham, A Parable of American Righteousness

Billy comes from a long line of evangelists who warned their listeners of the hell that awaited those who capitulate to sin. In America, the tradition reaches back to John Cotton and Cotton Mather, whose writings may have contributed to the Salem witchcraft trials, and Jonathan Edwards and his classic sermon "Sinners in the Hands of an Angry God." Then came Englishman George Whitefield, James McGready and the first camp meetings, and scholarly Charles Finney. Dwight L. Moody and then Billy Sunday brought the revivalist tradition up to Billy Graham. But unlike some of his predecessors, Billy emphasizes God's love rather than His wrath, His promises rather than His punishment. The twentieth century's premier evangelist was not, however, reluctant to name the sins he felt most virulent, including those to which he believed himself to be most vulnerable.

Several years ago Billy talked about temptation, saying, "I decided there were three areas that Satan could attack in—pride, morals, and finances. Over the years I tried to set up safeguards against the dangers of each.

"Take the third one, finances. In the early days I, like most other traveling evangelists, financed crusades by receiving love offerings. After a crusade like Los Angeles, Portland, or Atlanta, the people would give a love offering. . . . [Cliff] Barrows and I used to divide the love offering. I think the highest amount I ever got was eighteen thousand dollars. But that was big money in those days for two people just out of school. I knew I had to do something to protect us against misunderstandings about the love offerings."[1]

I find it amazing that Billy and his staff protected themselves against these temptations decades before the recent televangelists' scandals, and I raised this idea with him.

Frost: In 1948, early in your career, with extraordinary sort of farsightedness, given the history of evangelism and some of the more tawdry evangelists since, you had a Modesto Manifesto where you realized that far before the media were as powerful as they are today, that you had to protect yourself against the handling of money, being accused, immorality, and so on. What gave you that thought, years ahead of its time, really?

Graham: Well, I had had some role models that disappointed me in the way they lived and some of the things they did and some of the experiences they had that made newsprint, that hurt the cause of the kingdom of God and hurt our work. And I said, "Now we're going to take a pledge today that we're never going to engage in any of these things." And we took measures to be sure of that. For example, we now have a board of thirty-one top businessmen to run our business affairs, and I don't have anything to do with the finances of our organization, and we have taken steps in every direction we know and every area we know to prevent that.

Frost: And the remarkable thing is you did it forty-nine years ago.

Graham: That's right.

Frost: I mean, before these issues were really quite that clear.

Graham: Yes.[2]

Billy has honored this agreement through the years, but that doesn't stop the temptations. So I asked him, "What sort of temptations do you feel?"

Graham: The Bible says that Jesus Christ was tempted in all points like as we are, yet without sin. There are three main temptations that man has. There's the lust of the flesh. There's the lust of the eye. And there's the pride of life—in other words, ego. All three of these are temptations that Satan comes to us every day, tempting us in a thousand different ways and coming at us from different angles, but always using those three main avenues. This is what he used on Adam and Eve in the Garden of Eden. This is what he used on Jesus in the Mount of Temptation in the wilderness. And he hasn't changed his tactics. His tactics are still the same, and man is still falling for the same old arguments.

Frost: Which of the three does he go at you most with?

Graham: All three of them. Of course. I'm no exception. I mean, I couldn't say that I was better than my Lord, and the Pope would have to say the same. I mean, every one of us will have to confess these things, you see. . . . Now, it doesn't become sin to be tempted. Sin is when I yield to the temptation.

Frost: So it's not the thought necessarily . . . it's the commitment.

Graham: It's the mulling over the thought and sort of going over in my mind and saying, "My, I would enjoy . . ."

Frost: It's the enjoying the thought.

Graham: Yes, that's right. That's correct. That's the sin. And that's called in the Bible evil imagination. And that was one of the sins that led to the destruction of the human race.[3]

Or, as he once said, "A thought enters; we pamper it; it germinates and grows into an evil act."[4]

I recall Billy's response when asked about the very public falls of Jim and Tammy Bakker and Jimmy Swaggart. Billy is extremely consistent when it comes to the subject of temptation and sin. At that time he commented on their fall by saying, "We are all tempted. I think if they had realized what was happening and turned to the Lord in the deepest part of their lives, they would not have fallen. Of course, when a person becomes what [the Bakkers and Jimmy Swaggart] were on television and becomes a celebrity, he faces a special kind of temptation, a special time of vulnerability because you become a target for anybody who is jealous or anybody who is disloyal in the organization."[5]

Billy has done all he could over the years to avoid temptation. He says that to avoid sexual temptation he has never ridden alone in a car with a woman, or even eaten a meal alone with his secretary.[6]

But I still wondered. . . . "In what ways have you yielded to temptation?"

> **Graham:** I suppose, David, in almost every way. I have yielded, primarily in my thinking processes. I have never committed adultery. I have never, and I'm not saying it boastfully, I'm saying that because I think God kept me. I never touched a woman in the wrong way before I was married. I've never touched a woman in the wrong way. And I think God Himself has protected me. But there were times when the temptation was great. A few times. Especially since I've been married, when I traveled in other parts of the world. I

was with a friend of mine, who was a great Christian leader and he became so overwhelmed by temptation that he not only took cold showers, but he took the keys to his room and threw them out the window. It was in Paris. He didn't want to be able to get out of his room.

Frost: So that you've found those temptations, as you say, with travel and being a religious leader and so on, that you have been tempted by women through the years . . .

Graham: Yes.

Frost: But you've never succumbed?

Graham: No.

Frost: What temptations do you think you have yielded to?

Graham: I suppose that I have yielded to temptations of pride, though I'm not conscious of it, but I think I have. I think that is the number one sin that a man can have is pride. That was Satan's sin. That's the greatest sin. Idolatry and pride and they go together. I suppose there's been that, but I'm not conscious of it. Because today, I feel the opposite. I feel like I'm nothing but a worm crawling along the floor and shouldn't have any recognition from God at all, except judgment because I feel that my life has been a failure in many ways.[7]

Frost: You say in the big theological sense we're all sinners. . . . Can you think back, in addition to that, to little sins, too? I mean, the day when you borrowed some candies from a store that you weren't supposed to? I mean, can you think of little sins too, or—

Graham: Of course. I mean, all of us, I think, can. I think of a time right now, as you said, that I told my father a lie. That's always bothered me. In fact, it's bothered me very much, because it was quite a big lie that I told him at one time. . . .

And this was, of course, before my conversion to Christ. And I can think of all kinds of little things. Now, they would be little things compared to today's things, but this is not what God is alarmed about and what the Bible is about. Those are only symptoms of a disease that's deep inside. The real disease is a disease of blood pollution that we call "sin."[8]

Does Billy tackle the subjects of sin and temptation with the same gusto he did when he first walked the sawdust trail? I found his comments revealing: "I am preaching the same Gospel I have always preached. If anything, I am stressing more and more the cost of discipleship. I do not know of a single moral issue that I have not spoken out on at one time or another—everything from racism and apartheid to nuclear armaments and peace. However, I do not feel it is my calling to get out in the streets and lead demonstrations. Nor am I singling out one sin from the scores mentioned in Scripture and riding a hobbyhorse—although I have had a lot of pressure across the years to do so. . . .

"There is a difference between *sin* and *sins*. There is *sin* (singular), which is the heart of our spiritual disease, and there are *sins* (plural), which are the fruit or signs of the disease. If I spent all of my time on *sins* (plural) I might never be able to get at the root cause, which is *sin* (singular). The Lord Jesus Christ died on the cross to deal with sin and not just individual *sins*."[9]

On the topic of sin (singular) and evil, I asked Billy, "Have you ever met anybody who you've thought, 'There is an evil man'?"

Graham: No. Perhaps I'm too easygoing, and perhaps I

think too good of everybody. I really do love everybody. I have not met anybody that I didn't like and didn't love. And I have seen pictures of Eichmann and Hitler and people like that, and I'm sure there are thousands of those like that today that I believe are dominated by evil. But even that I think is a power outside themselves. I've seen on the television screen some of these people that I think are evil, but I think there's a supernatural evil power that's dominating them. And in Jesus' day they would call it demon possession.

Frost: But none of them were born evil, you wouldn't have thought?

Graham: Yes, we're all born with a tendency to evil. I mean, we all have the seed of evil within us, of hate and lust and greed, and that's called original sin.[10]

Billy recently said, "Everything comes from the human heart, and our hearts have been corrupted by sin. And the only answer to sin, in my judgment, is Christ."[11]

He receives many letters, and the writers often ask about sin and temptation. A typical letter from a young woman asks, "How can I handle sex?" Billy's response sounds a lot like what he's said to me and many other interviewers over the years: "Acknowledge that sex is an important part of life, but that it is far from being the *most* important. Accept sex as God given and thank Him for it. But remember that every gift carries a burden of responsibility. This needs self-discipline: chastity before marriage, fidelity afterwards.

"Ask Christ to help you with your sex problems. The Bible says that He was 'tempted in every point,' just as you are tempted. His strength to resist temptation is available to you."[12]

For the thousands who write in with questions like these, Billy says, "I ask my correspondents to go to the inspired Word of God to find a foundation for their behavior."[13]

His bottom-line answer about sin is, "Our fellowship with [God] is broken when we tolerate sin in our lives."[14] But I wondered about areas that aren't as clearly right or wrong—at least according to some people.

"What about alcohol?" I inquired of Billy Graham. "I know you don't drink. Would you classify taking a drink as a sin? A lot of Christians do."

Graham: I don't think that the Bible teaches teetotalism. When the Bible says that Jesus turned water into wine, that wasn't grape juice in my judgment. That was wine, the best wine. And I think that the Scripture teaches in the last chapter of Proverbs, for example, when a person has troubles in an old age and so forth that it's good to take some alcohol. Or it says—Paul was writing to Timothy and said take a little wine for your stomach's sake. You'd be amazed at how many people have stomach trouble and use that to justify it, you see.

But the reason that I don't, David, is because I feel that I have another principle at work. The Bible says, if I do anything to make my brother stumble or fall, then I'm not to do it. And if people saw me sitting at a table drinking (alcohol) in America at least—then they may say, "Well, Billy Graham does it; it's all right for me," and they may become an alcoholic as a result of that. So I have to be careful of my witness.[15]

Billy once said, "It is no sin to be rich, but it is sinful to trust in riches and think they bring security."[16] That prompted me to ask, "Have you ever felt temptations about money?"

> **Frost:** It's very normal for people to suggest that you're a millionaire, and so on, and I know that you're not and that you take a fixed salary, don't you, from your evangelistic association. And I know, also, it's very fashionable for evangelists to say that money is the root of all evil, period. But are there things that you're glad that you've got the money to buy?
>
> **Graham:** Yes, I'm glad that I can give my family a home, and I'm glad that I can give them good food. I'm glad that I can give them an education and those things that I think all of us want for our families. And I think that I'm also glad that I was able to purchase a television set so we could watch the Beatles.[17]

And on another occasion:

> **Graham:** No, I never have [been tempted by money].
> **Frost:** I don't think you have.
> **Graham:** I don't know why, but I determined years ago that I was not going to go for money. I've never been interested in money, except as it pays our expenses and bills and things like that. And my wife and I could have been millionaires many times over. We've been offered everything you can think of, and we have said no to all of them.[18]

Yet no amount of precautions can eliminate all rumors of indiscretion for someone as well known and easily recognized as Billy Graham. Two of my favorite stories about his daughter Bunny and longtime colleague George Beverly Shea illustrate the point. Billy says, "I remember walking down the street in New York with my beautiful blond daughter, Bunny. I was holding her hand. I heard somebody behind us say, 'There goes Billy Graham with one of those blond girls.'"[19]

Once in Germany, "Bev Shea, Cliff Barrows, and I went out to eat at a restaurant. The next day the papers reported that 'Billy Graham ate at a restaurant last evening in the company of a woman named Beverly Shea.'"[20]

Playing devil's advocate, I once observed that Billy and his entourage like good things. "You stay in good hotels, eat in fine restaurants and travel to England on the *Queen Mary*," I suggested. With trademark wit and humor, Graham answered:

Graham: When I came over to England in 1954 for a crusade at Harringay Arena and Wembley Stadium, I was asked at a press conference why I didn't travel like Jesus. Why would I come on this big, beautiful, luxurious *Queen Mary*? And I said, "Well, Jesus traveled on a donkey; you find me a donkey that can swim the Atlantic, and I'll try to buy him."

Frost: But no one's come up with one yet?

Graham: No, I haven't found a donkey that could swim the Atlantic. So I'm afraid I'm going to have to continue to use the airlines and the ships.[21]

Endnotes

1. Myra, Harold. "William Franklin Graham: Seventy Exceptional Years." *Christianity Today*, November 18, 1988, 21.

2. "Reverend Billy Graham talking with David Frost," PBS, May 30, 1997.

3. "The David Frost Show," Westinghouse Broadcasting, 1970.

4. *The Billy Graham Christian Workers Handbook* (Minneapolis: World Wide Publications, 1984).

5. Aikman, David. "Preachers, Politics and Temptation." *Time*, May 28, 1990, 13.

6. Ibid.

7. "Reverend Billy Graham talking with David Frost," PBS, January 23, 1993.

8. "The David Frost Show," Westinghouse Broadcasting, 1969.

9. "Candid Conversation with the Evangelist." *Christianity Today*, July 17, 1981, 21.

10. "The David Frost Show," Westingouse Broadcasting, 1970.

11. Cal Thomas on CNBC, May 5, 1996.

12. Graham, Billy. "Some Tormenting Questions for Our Time." *Reader's Digest*, April 1972, 82.

13. *Ibid.*

14. "Candid Conversation with the Evangelist." In *Christianity Today*, July 17, 1981, 21.

15. "The David Frost Show," Westinghouse Broadcasting, 1970.

16. Covington, Roy. "Covetousnous Is America's Greatest Sin, Says Graham." *Charlotte Observer*, September 25, 1958.

17. "Doubts and Certainties: David Frost interview with Billy Graham," BBC-2, 1964.

18. "Reverend Billy Graham Talking with David Frost," PBS, January 23, 1993.

19. Myra, Harold. "William Franklin Graham: Seventy Exceptional Years." *Christianity Today*, November 18, 1988, 23.

20. *Ibid*

21. "The David Frost Show," Westinghouse Broadcasting, 1970.

CHAPTER 8

Billy Graham
on
Moral and Social Issues

If you go to the streets your people will desert you, and you won't have the opportunity to have integrated crusades.

Martin Luther King, Jr.
Advice to Billy Graham

*T*hough Billy's ministry has maintained a tight evangelical focus on the Gospel of Jesus Christ, his worldwide prominence has made him a ready source for the media whenever it needs a Christian perspective on the social and moral issues of our time. And he has not been a reluctant commentator, applying God's Word—as he sees it—to contemporary ethics and mores. I think he best summedup his reason for this outspokenness when he said, "The most prominent place in hell is reserved for those who are neutral on the great issues of life."[1]

Although born in the South, Billy grew up in a tolerant environment. The foreman of his family's farm, Reese Brown, was black and treated like a family member. From his first crusades in the north, where reporters assumed he was racist, Billy responded, "All men are created equal under God. Any denial of that is contradiction of holy law."[2] It's been said of him that he "could imagine no route to racial harmony that did not run past the cross."[3]

As early as 1952, he told a crusade audience, "It may be there are places where [separation] is desirable to both races, but certainly not in the church."[4] More recently he's reiterated his position by saying "Of all people, Christians should be the most active in reaching out to those of other races."[5] And on another occasion: "We're suffering from only one disease in the world. Our basic problem is not a race problem. . . . Our basic problem is a heart problem. We need to get the heart changed, the heart transformed."[6]

Billy and I have explored this topic over the years. On the international scene, he told me in 1970 why he had never preached in South Africa.

> **Graham:** I've never been to South Africa. I've been invited many times but felt that I couldn't go because I've had a policy of never preaching to segregated audiences. I wouldn't even want to go and preach in areas where even a permit had to be made. . . .
>
> We might consider an invitation. Because I'm told by some of my friends that have been there that the situation has, in some areas, been exaggerated and that it is possible to hold integrated meetings in South Africa in some areas. . . . But I don't think anyone anywhere in the world can possibly excuse apartheid.[7]

In 1973, Billy did hold a crusade in South Africa—the first major public interracial gathering in the nation. I later noted that the world had changed and Billy's attitude toward the world had also changed. He agreed and began talking about Nelson Mandela.

> **Graham:** I received a note from [Mandela] in which he invited me to come and see him. He said that about three or four years ago, he had received Christ into his heart. He was reading and studying the Bible. There's a man in my home state that has been helping him a great deal, and he was the contact between us. I was planning, about a year ago, to go see [Mandela] and then certain things intervened that I could not go see him, but I had hoped to see him.[8]

I still find Billy speaking out about racism: "Racial and ethnic hostility is the foremost social problem facing our world today. From the systematic horror of 'ethnic cleansing' in Bosnia to the random violence savaging our inner cities, our world seems caught up in a tidal wave of racial and ethnic tension. This hostility threatens the very foundations of modern society.

"We must not underestimate the devastating effects of racism on our world. Daily headlines chronicle its grim toll: divided nations and families, downward spiral of poverty and hopelessness, children cruelly broken in body and warped in heart and mind. The list is long, but for the sensitive Christian, it is even longer: whole peoples poisoned by violence and racial hatred and closed to the Gospel as a result; indifference and resistance by Christians who are intolerant toward those of other backgrounds, ignoring their spiritual and physical needs. . . .

"Tragically, too often in the past evangelical Christians have turned a blind eye to racism or have been willing to stand aside while others take the lead on racial reconciliation, saying it was not our responsibility. (I admit I share in that blame.) As a result, many efforts toward reconciliation in America have lacked a Christian foundation and may not outlive the immediate circumstances that brought them into existence. Our consciences should be stirred to repentance by how far we have fallen short of what God asks us to be as His agents of reconciliation."[9]

Here, again in 1970, he talked to me about race relations in the United States:

Graham: One of the things that disturbs me in the United States at the moment is there's a certain element in the black community, a small element to be sure, that wants separatism. . . . For example, I know a university right now where the dormitories are completely integrated, but where the blacks are saying, "No, we want our own dormitory; we want our own classes; we want separatism." Now, whether this is going to be the beginning of something that will grow, I hope not, because I think the only hope for America to settle her race problem is an integrated society.

But there are those today that don't agree with that, in the black community as well as the white community, and whether they will gain momentum or not, I don't know.

Frost: How do you think the battle against racism is going basically?

Graham: I think it's going better in the South than it is in the north. I think Martin Luther King was correct when he evaluated several years ago that the problem in the South would be solved much before—a much longer time before the north. Because, you see, in the South you have great personal friendships between black and white. The blacks hardly know the whites in the north—except in certain top circles. But I have many friends among black people that have moved from the South to the north that have already moved back because they don't like it in the north. They feel there's a hypocrisy in the north. And we had what was called *de jure* segregation in the South, which has been completely done away with. But we never really faced up to *de facto* segregation which you have in the northern part of the United States.

So I would say that in the major cities of the north is where the explosions, if there are any—and God forbid that there will be any more—where the explosions may occur. And that's the reason that this next year in our crusading we're concentrating in cities in the north for major crusades like Cleveland and Chicago and Oakland, California, where there's been—and Berkeley—that area where there's been a lot of disturbance and where the headquarters of the Black Panthers are. And we're going to hold crusades in those cities next year, hoping that our meetings may have some healing effect. Because through television and the mass media, these big crowds, we can say something to a local community. [10]

When the nation was deeply divided by many issues in 1970, I asked Billy how much a president can do to bring the nation together, which led to his thoughts on extremists.

Graham: I think he can do a great deal. He can. But I don't think we're going to be brought together quite like that. It seems to me that we've got extremists, David, the extreme right and the extreme left that are almost irreconcilable. And we've got a group of people now that really believe in the violent overthrow of the government. Now, they do not have any system that they would like to substitute. They've come forward with no plan as yet; they just want to destroy. And I don't know whether you can carry on a dialogue with this type of person or not. I don't— some of them I know. They'll talk to me; some of them will. And I have met with them several times. And I just find that it's almost impossible to reason. They're not interested in reason. They're not interested in dialogue. They're not interested in sitting down quietly and talking about the problem. They're interested in disruption, in violence, in destruction to bring down the system.

Frost: But then, if you come in a little from that, to on the one hand people like hard hats and on the other hand, you know, protesting students who are protesting violently, but really passionately against the system in some way or another, how do you bring those two groups together? I mean, given that you'll never bring a Ku Klux Klan man together with a really violent Weatherman? You know what I mean. But how do you bring closer together a right-wing hard hat and a left-wing student?

Graham: I would doubt if we could ever get them to agree, but we can get them to agree, "Well, let's work for change"—as from their point of view—"within the system." Because I don't think there's ever been a system devised that's absolutely perfect in history. And America probably has come as close to it, I think the British have come as close to it as any other system, but none of them are perfect.

And could we bring this change that's desperately needed? We all know there's a need in change in educational system, in social justice. We shouldn't have ghettoes in modern America. This should be eliminated. But can we bring this about within the Constitution, within the framework of government, rather than tearing the whole thing down, having total chaos and then a dictatorship coming and taking over? Because that's exactly what would happen. If we destroy the system, a dictator is going to rise—either a right-winger or a left-winger.[11]

Billy did not take a strong public stand on the U.S. involvement in Vietnam. When asked why, he said, "I don't intend to make any [statement] because I really don't know the answer to these complicated political questions. Some questions, let us say like the race question which is to me a very moral question, I can take a very strong stand on because I believe I know the answer to that. . . . I find in the United States that equally devout Christians are on both sides of the Vietnam question, and I am not sure exactly what is the answer.[12]

And, "I just decided that this was such a divisive and emotional issue in America that my job was to preach the Gospel to the people on both sides. If I took a stand on one of these sides or the other, half the people would not hear what I was saying about Christ."[13]

Certainly among evangelicals, Billy was a bellwether when it came to rapprochement with communists. I once inquired when the evangelist realized he must make a bridge to the communist world.

> **Graham:** This came about through a long period of prayer and Bible study. I began to realize that God had not called anyone just to the Anglo-Saxon world or just to the white people of the world. But we're called to the whole world, regardless of political ideology or race or whatever. And I remember struggling with that before I made the decision to go. . . . I'd already been to communist countries— but to go to Russia to address a peace conference [in 1982], which in those days looked like a betrayal of all that we stood for in America.[14]

During one show, I aired a tape excerpt of Senator Mark Hatfield assessing Billy's mission to the Soviet Union. Then Billy talked to me about his decision to make the trip even though it was controversial.

Hatfield: We had discussions over a period of time about his dream that I believe started in 1959 to go to the Soviet Union, to preach the Gospel to the Soviets, to preach it in all parts of the world, not just the Soviet Union. That offered that greatest challenge because of the political system. And we discussed it and he was very realistic. I suggested at times, "You will get the strongest criticism from the Christian right because they will feel somehow that you're compromising with the Devil."

Graham: I knew it was going to be highly controversial. So on the Sunday before I went, George Bush invited me to lunch at his home, because we'd been friends for many years. And before the lunch, he said, "You know, I don't think the Reagans have anybody here . . . and I think I'm going to call them and see if they'll come over."

He called them and they came over, President and Mrs. Reagan. I said, "Mr. President, I'm going, as you know, to Moscow to speak at a peace conference and," I said, "I know your stand on this and you probably know mine." "Oh," he said, "don't worry about it." He said, "It will come out all right." He said, "I'm going to be praying for you." Neither one of them said don't go. Neither of them even hinted that I shouldn't go.[15]

"How do you decide whether people are trying to use you and whether you can use the opportunity more than they can try to use you?" I asked.

Graham: Oh, I knew that they were trying to use me, but I wanted to be used in the sense that I wanted my message on peace to go out, but I also wanted to open doors and they have opened throughout the Eastern world, and I knew that if I went to the peace conference, I would have an opportunity to preach the Gospel later on because in my acceptance of that responsibility, I was virtually promised that doors would be opened.

And now I've had the privilege of preaching the Gospel in various parts of the Soviet Union, all the Eastern countries except Bulgaria, and we have an invitation now to Bulgaria. And I think that—now, for example, my next meetings will be in the People's Stadium in Hungary and Budapest, and that's a stadium that's larger than Wembley.

Frost: So that as opposed to what we all thought years ago, you think that Christianity and communism can coexist in a country?

Graham: Of course. They're doing it in the Eastern world now and the church is getting stronger in those countries, as it is in China, incidentally, in spite of all these difficulties.

Frost: Do you think that the Eastern European countries invite you in order to try and get you to give a "Good Housekeeping Seal of Approval" to them?

Graham: I don't know why I'm invited, but whatever it is, I preach the Gospel.[16]

In 1982 and 1985, Billy got his chance to preach in the Soviet Union, much to the chagrin of some who rued his doing business with communists. He answered his critics this way, speaking of his first trip: "In all, I gave over fifty sermons, lectures, and speeches—the most intensive schedule in my entire forty years of ministry. . . .

A high point was my sermon at the Church of the Epiphany in Moscow, the most important Orthodox church in the country. It was packed with people, and I preached on how to be born again—the same message I give everywhere I go. . . . I took advantage of that one moment when they invited me, and now they have invited me to come back. . . .

"I thought it was worth taking [the risk I was being used] for the sake of preaching the Gospel and, secondly, for the cause of world peace."[17]

"Free love" was the way people were describing the new sexual morality of the sixties. Billy, of course, took a dim view of profligate sexual practices. "But aren't you saying the act of lovemaking is solely for procreation?" I once questioned.

Graham: I would say that it's intended partially for pleasure as well, but within the restrictions laid down in the Scriptures. I believe the Bible teaches that fornication and adultery are sins, that we will be held accountable to God. But it's rather interesting, in studying this and the life of Christ, how He dealt with it. He dealt rather gently with it, and He forgave.

And I think that when we come and repent of our sin, whatever it may be, that He does forgive. But we have had such a hush-hush attitude about sex and especially in Britain and America, and we went back to the old Victorian and puritanic times, and I think that this was a mistake. It should be out in the open. It's in the open in the Bible. The ministers should have been talking about it all along, telling young people what is right and what is wrong, you see.

Frost: In making hard and fast statements about what is right and what is wrong, do you think that whether a thing is right or wrong is changed by the motives behind it?

Graham: I don't agree that the Bible, in any way, condones a prostitute, let's say, giving herself to a man and saying that in doing so, she's actually serving God, as someone has suggested. I don't believe that the Bible teaches that at all.

Frost: You talk simply about adultery and fornication being wrong. Well, it's just wrong. That's fair enough, but it seems to me that the motives make a great deal of difference.

Graham: Well, what is the motive, for example?

Frost: There's a difference between making love, for instance, as an expression of love and not as an expression of love, isn't there?

Graham: I'm not sure that it's the kind of love we're talking about, you see. The love in the Scriptures that we have from Christ is *agape* love, which Christ gives to every one of us and gives us a capacity to love, and I believe that the Bible teaches that only the true believer in Christ has the capacity to really love, that is, with a depth of love.

And this is the evil, it seems to me, of fornication and these things because it breaks that bond of love and it also hinders—I've talked to many psychologists at this point—it hinders real love within marriage.

Frost: But not always does it destroy real love, does it? Not always?

Graham: I don't know that it always destroys, but it always hurts and blunts real love, yes, always.

Frost: Surely there are couples everywhere—I mean, I'm not particularly speaking just for the other side, but there are couples everywhere who disprove that simple statement, don't they, that it always blunts?

Graham: No, because I think that almost every psychologist that I've talked to—these great psychologists in America and they all agree that at this point when a person goes beyond their own standards, that it leaves psychological reactions. And secondly, that within the bonds of matrimony, that love is blunted if one has been promiscuous before marriage.[18]

During a subsequent interview, we continued our discussion on the place of sex in marriage, including the issue of birth control, on which Billy has also spoken out. He has said, "I am a strong advocate of birth control. . . . I don't think it should ever be a state control. I don't think we should ever set a limit on families and say that no family can have more than two or three children. I think that it has to be voluntary."[19] When we talked about it he expanded on this:

Graham: I don't think there's anything in the Bible that teaches that sex is just for the propagation of the race. Sex is to be enjoyment within marriage. It's to be the fulfillment of the marriage bond and not just to produce children.

And I think that, when one travels in India and one goes to the Orient and sees this pressure of population—in this country alone—let's take the United States. In six generations, if the present population increase continues, do you know how many people will be in the United States? Nine billion in six generations at the present increase. . . .

But we know that human nature cannot live that close together. This is going to bring about explosions. It's going to bring about famines. It's going to bring about war. It's going to bring about all kinds of problems. And we're rushing madly toward them now. We need some form of family planning and birth control.[20]

Recently I brought up the subject of cloning.

Frost: How do you feel reading all these stories about cloning sheep and maybe cloning people, so that if you'd been around for a few more years, we could have cloned Billy Graham, and [your son] Franklin never would have gotten the job? Do you think that it is man playing God, or do you welcome it?

Graham: No. I think it's man playing God, and I think it's a terrible thing. And I don't think it will ever be [succesful] as far as humans are concerned. How can man clone, for example, the love that a person has for another person. And, of course, Jesus said, "By this shall all men know that you're my followers and that you love one another." And the greatest need we have in the world today is love and understanding between people based on that kind of love. And in Greek the word for that kind of love is a very deep word, not the physical love, but our God-given love, *agape*. And we love each other as believers, but we love the whole world that way. And God loved the whole world that way because that's why He gave Christ to die on the cross.[21]

Finally, our conversation about the end of the twentieth century sums up Billy's thoughts on the state of the world.

Frost: Tell me, what do you think is the greatest moral issue that we face in the twenty-first century?

Graham: Well, of course I would have to say sin.

Frost: Right, sin first. . . . The twentieth century has seen marvelous technological developments, and so on, and marvelous new forms of healing and there are plusses, and so on, but do the minuses outweigh the plusses?

Graham: I think they do. I think that technologically we're tremendous and we've got so much technology that the average person doesn't know anything about what's being developed at this moment that will absolutely change communications, for example, this communication, television. I think that this is a bad thing because it's bringing into our homes not only the good things, but all the terrible things, and young people seem to be more impressed with the bad than with the good. And I think that this is a very bad thing. You can get things tonight on television, especially late at night, that you're just watching in the bedroom and you see everything. Well, you know, this would shake a young person. A lot of them stay up late at night to see that.

Frost: So that makes you a pessimist about the new millenium, or an optimist?

Graham: I'm an optimist because I know what the end is going to be. The end is going to be that Christ is going to come and rule the world.[22]

Endnotes

1. Quotable Quotes. *Reader's Digest*, February 1972, 69.

2. Martin, William. *A Prophet with Honor: The Billy Graham Story* (New York: William Morrow, 1991), 169.

3. *Ibid.*

4. Gilbreath, Edward. "Billy Graham Had a Dream." *Christian History*, no. 47: 46.

5. *Ibid.*

6. "For the Living of These Days." *The Cumberland Presbyterian*, February 15, 1972.

7. "The David Frost Show," Westinghouse Broadcasting, 1970.

8. "Frost on Sunday: Interview with Billy Graham," TV-am, Great Britain, 1989.

9. Graham, Billy. "Racism and the Evangelical Church." *Christianity Today*, October 4, 1993, 27.

10. "The David Frost Show," Westinghouse Broadcasting, 1970.

11. *Ibid.*

12. "Meet Billy Graham." *The Christian and Christianity Today*, June 10, 1966, 21.

13. Wakin, Edward. "Revival Tents and Golden Domes." *U.S. Catholic*, March 1976, 10.

14. "Reverend Billy Graham talking with David Frost," PBS, January 29, 1993.

15. "A Prophet with Honor: David Frost documentary on Billy Graham," Channel Four, Great Britain, 1989.

16. *Ibid.*

17. "100 Million in the Soviet Union Profess Belief in God." *U.S. News & World Report*, October 8, 1984, 38

18. "Doubts and Certainties: David Frost interview with Billy Graham," BBC-2, 1964.

19. "Billy Graham, The Man at Home." *The Saturday Evening Post*, Spring 1972, 16.

20. "The David Frost Show," Westinghouse Broadcasting, 1969.

21. "Reverend Billy Graham talking with David Frost," PBS, May 30, 1997.

22. *Ibid.*

CHAPTER 9

Billy Graham
on
Billy Graham

If You let me serve You with that man I'd consider it the greatest privilege of my life.

A conversation Ruth Bell had with God about fellow student Billy Graham.

*W*hen it comes to personal matters, personal feelings, and personal opinions, Billy is admittedly not as forthcoming as he once was. Unlike his bride, Ruth, whom interviewers adore because she is so open and quotable, the evangelist has learned to be more circumspect, especially when the subject is open to debate even among Christians. He has said, "I used to talk on every subject. If somebody asked me anything political I'd talk on it. I've learned through the years that I'm much better off keeping quiet on certain subjects in order that I may appeal to a wider group of people in my presentation of the Gospel."[1] But on those subjects Billy will talk about, I find him most forthcoming.

In one of our conversations, I suggested he took a giant step forward when he learned to say, "'I don't know,' because there are certain things we don't know."

> **Graham:** That's right.
>
> **Frost:** That's a development over the years, isn't it? At the beginning of your mission, you probably would have had an answer for everything, wouldn't you?
>
> **Graham:** Yes, probably out of ignorance or lack of study or lack of world travel and meeting with leaders all over the world. I've learned that there are some things I do not understand, certain things in the Bible I don't understand. And I leave that to God. Someday I'll understand them.[2]

I also wondered, as he looked back over his life, if there were statements that he made that now cause him to blush a little.

Graham: Yes. There are many statements, David, I wish I had never made, and I think this happens to everyone later in life, because you become, I hope, more mature and you learn a great deal. And in one's travels and contacts and reading, you learn.

For example, I made the statement many years ago—the actual dimensions of heaven.

Frost: Sixteen hundred miles in each direction.

Graham: You have a very good memory. I didn't know you knew that I made it. And many statements like that that were rather foolish that I made, and I wouldn't make today.[3]

Billy is one of the best-read men I know. Just listen to his reading list for current events: "I take several newspapers: the *New York Times, Washington Post, Charlotte Observer, Asheville Citizen, Wall Street Journal, London Times*—daily as well as the Sunday *Times*. I also take the [*London*] *Mail*, which gives me more of the other side of British political thinking. Then I take the *Telegraph* and the *London Observer*, which is a weekly.

"Of course, people here help me read them and check things they think I ought to read. But I get the whole paper, and most days I at least thumb through them all. Ruth reads everything, too. She's my number-one source of knowledge in some areas.

"And then, of course, we get *Time, Newsweek*, and *U.S. News & World Report*. The only Christian magazine that I really read is *Christianity Today*; I also take the *Christian Century*."[4]

No wonder the Graham children were impressed by their father's attention to study when he came home from crusades! He told me about his study habits:

Graham: I study almost all the time. My children said, "Daddy, we thought when we finished school, that we'd finished studying, but you study more than we do." I have to study, I have to keep up with current events. I have to keep up with theological trends. I have to keep up with trends in philosophy and psychology and all these related fields.

Frost: How much of the day do you spend reading the Bible?

Graham: Every morning I read five psalms and I read one chapter of Proverbs. That's been a longtime policy of mine and practice, and I have my devotions. And then after breakfast when I'm home, if I don't—I don't have any appointments in the morning, I spend another half an hour just reading the Bible without studying, just reading, just filling my soul, because I've found that I like to preach from an overflow. I like to read myself full and then preach from that rather than just certain prepared sermons on certain topics. My sermons are not like the ordinary sermons. I don't have too many firstlys, secondlys, and thirdlys and fourthlys. Sometimes I have as many as seventeen points to a sermon. . . . It's very much like the old Puritans used to preach, you know. They'd preach all these various things all in one sermon.

Frost: With that much reading of it, I know how you feel it's the Word of God and so on, but do you, in simple human terms, ever get bored with the Bible?

Graham: Never.

Frost: Honestly?

Graham: Honestly.

Frost: You must do sometimes.

Graham: Honestly.

Frost: Some of those chapters in Leviticus, and so on?

Graham: No, because they're all very important once you understand what it's all about. I mean, all of these were types of Christ and His coming and prepared the way for His coming. Even the begets—you know, so-and-so beget so-and-so. Well, that used to be very boring to me, but now they're quite exciting because they are tracing many times the lineage of Jesus right on down and many of these people were in his background and each one was important. Now, for example, I remember that when Cecil B. DeMille was making *The Ten Commandments*, he asked me to come out and review it to see what I thought about it.

I said, "Mr. DeMille, there's one interesting scene here. Here are the people going out of Israel. Now," I said, "you have one Egyptian there. Where do you find in the Bible that an Egyptian was leaving?" And he turned me over to 2 Chronicles to a very obscure passage where Moses' foster mother went out with him. Now, I had never seen that passage before and yet, Mr. DeMille had seen it and put it in his film.

Frost: I got the impression from his films that he never read the Bible at all, in fact.

Graham: Oh, he was a great Bible student. We just did his life story on television in America, and I had the privilege of participating in that. I was very close friends with Mr. DeMille because in—let's see—1950, he asked me if I would go into films and I said no. God had called me to preach.[5]

On his role as father, I asked if because of his heavy travel schedule, he had short-changed his children. I knew, of course, of his son Franklin's rebellious teenage years, of which Billy has said, "We knew he'd get over that. . . . We were in prayer for him all the time, and I never rebuked him. I never tried to get him to change his ways. I just prayed for him and loved him. I think love is the thing that young people are looking for today." [6]

Frost: But you feel, in a sense, that your ministry short-changed your five children as a father a bit?

Graham: It did. I think that . . . I don't think that any of the children would say that. But, I feel it. I feel, I feel the emptiness of not being as much of a confidant that I would like to be to my two sons and three daughters.

Frost: That was a sacrifice you made, in a sense, for the mission, for the cause, for the crusade.

Graham: That's correct. [7]

I once asked Billy Graham, "What do you do when you're not reading the Bible or studying?" I know he doesn't want people to put him on a pedestal. He has said, "They think that I live a saintly life all the time, that I read the Bible and pray full-time and that's just not true." [8]

Graham: I have my family. Of course, I enjoy my family. I have five children; I have a grandson now [in 1964]. And I play golf. I play—it's three miles to the golf course and I try to play in the summer almost every day that I'm home for nine holes, at least. I lift weights. I keep in as good a physical condition as I possibly can. I climb a mountain every day. I live in the mountains, and there's a mountain back of me that takes about a half an hour to go up and down. So that helps keep me in condition. And then I'm busy in my work the rest of the time because I'm writing. I love to write.

Frost: To what extent do you participate in the sort of conventional time-spendings of going out to dinner, watching television, going to the ball game or—

Graham: I'm quite a baseball fan and we do go to ball games once in a while, and I do watch certain television programs. I have certain ones that I watch and certain ones that I don't. I never watch on Sunday, but I do watch some during the week. I watch the news programs because they come on in America at 6:30 each evening for a half an hour and I watch that. I read the news magazines. I read the daily press. I get three newspapers from London, which I scan every day that I'm home. . . . I get a great deal of my preaching material from the London press.[9]

"In one interview, you said you regard yourself as a failure," I reminded Billy. "Do you believe that?"

Graham: Yes, when it comes to many areas, David, I do feel that I could have done so much more had I studied more or gone further in school, probably spent more time with my family. I have spent so little time with my family. And, thank God, they're all wonderful children and wonderful grandchildren. But I attribute that largely to the fact that Ruth dedicated her life to the family, while I dedicated my life to the ministry. But Ruth had been a great help in my ministry as well.[10]

In another interview, I asked about how he grew up—which included the evangelist-to-be as a milkman and door-to-door salesman.

Graham: I used to deliver milk, you see. My father was a dairy farmer and we used to deliver milk early in the morning. . . . I remember one night when about three in the morning I was delivering milk and the snow had fallen, and a dog got after me. And I ran in a direction that I had never taken before to get back to the milk truck. And a wire had been strung—a clothes wire had been strung, and it caught me right in the neck, and I did a double twist, and it almost severed my head from the body. I'll never forget that. And the dog came on top of that and attacked me while I was down.

Frost: Is that the point you decided to give up being a milkman?

Graham: No, I decided that the first day I had to milk cows. I used to have to milk before I went to school in the morning. And then I'd have to milk those same cows when I came home in the afternoon. And I decided in those days that I thought there were other things in life that I could do rather than milking cows. But that's not the reason I went into the ministry, because when I went into the ministry, I had often said that there are two things that I'll never do. One is to be an undertaker, and the other is to be a clergyman. I put them both in the same category. Two things I didn't want to be.

Frost: When was it that in order to raise a little money for your studies you sold brushes?

Graham: I sold brushes from door-to-door in the Depression trying to make enough money to help in my schooling. My father helped me, too. But he didn't help me enough. And so I went at it with all the zest that I could and would work from morning until night selling brushes. And my technique was to always offer the lady a free brush. And, of course, in those days that appealed. And then I would have to empty my whole case of brushes to get to the bottom, you see, to give this free brush. And the woman's curiosity by that time would be looking at these brushes, and she would say, "By the way, what is this, and how much is that?" Well, I knew I had a fish, you see, on the string by that time.

And then if that didn't work, many times you'd go to the door and the lady would come and just crack the door, and I knew that the door was soon going to slam, so I always put my foot in there, you see, and would say—and talk her into this free brush. "No, I'm not here really to sell you anything. I'm here to give you a brush. Just a gift. Just let me give you the brush." "Well, all right." Some of the biggest sales were made that way.[11]

Billy's success as a salesman prompted me to ask for his definition of the word *success*. In past interviews he had said he didn't feel successful as a college president, for example. He admitted, "I wasn't a very good president. I felt called of God [to become an evangelist]."[12]

Frost: I was talking to an American, and we got on to talking about you. . . . He said to me, "Well, I don't care whether Dr. Graham is an evangelist or an oil millionaire, or whatever. What I admire about Dr. Graham is that he's successful in whatever he does." Now, what, in fact, to you is being successful?

Graham: I would say that the word *success* may be

totally different in the sight of God than it is in the sight of the newspapers or people such as you've quoted, because perhaps the man in the small parish that is serving God faithfully every day, or perhaps the scrubwoman or perhaps the factory worker who is serving God in their own way as best they know how may be far more successful than I am.

And when I stand at the gate of heaven, I'm not going to say, "Lord, let me in because I've preached to great crowds." My only hope of getting into heaven is the cross of Christ and the mercy and the grace of God.[13]

Naturally, his theology has been put under the microscope constantly as people try to discern shifts in Billy's positions on both religious and secular matters. In that context, I inquired if he was a "fundamentalist."

Graham: I would not call myself today a fundamentalist, because it carries with it the weight of the publicity that has surrounded the word fundamentalist of being obscurantist, of being an extremist, of holding certain social views that I do not hold. And fundamentalists are looked upon as people who are more or less behind the times. I've tried to be contemporary. I've tried to keep up with what's going on in the world and relate my messages to the world. For example, any event that's going on in the world that is making the news, I use it as a springboard for my message because that's what the people are thinking about.[14]

Later we talked again about the difference between fundamentalists and evangelicals. That led to Billy's talking about Catholics and Protestants as well.

Frost: There is a division between those two words [evangelical and fundamentalist] that people still don't altogether understand.

Graham: Well, it's certainly true here in this country. There's a difference between the fundamentalist, who is a person who takes a stand on certain controversial issues and won't move from that stand and there's an intolerance, and I felt that God had called me to love all people, whatever church they went to, whether it's Catholic or Protestant or whomever, and work with them. And today we have almost 100 percent Catholic support in this country. That was not true even twenty years ago. And the bishops and archbishops and the Pope are our friends and we have plans underway now for a couple events that will probably be world news about our relationship with the Roman Catholic Church, because there's so much have in common and so much of what we believe. They believe in Christ. They believe in the death of Christ on the cross and His resurrection, and there are some other areas that there are differences.

Frost: Like confession or something?

Graham: Well, confessing to a priest, but we all confess, or we need to anyway, to God.

Frost: To God. You go direct, you go direct.

Graham: Go direct.[15]

I find interviewing Billy Graham endlessly fascinating. We never have enough time to cover all of the subjects that I'd like to ask him about. Any of his wide-ranging comments could be the basis of another interview. For example—

On preaching and his health: "There are times when I've come down from the platform absolutely exhausted. I feel like I've been wrestling with the Devil."[16] And, "I can tell that I'm seventy-five [1994] in some ways, but in other ways I feel like I'm twenty-five."[17]

On another Billy Graham: "God will raise up different ones who will do far better than me."[18]

On our generation's fascination with angels: "We have a community of devils, and Satan is their commander-in-chief. Jesus is the commander-in-chief of the angels. They are very powerful—not all powerful—and do God's bidding. I believe we have guardian angels. I expect I would have been dead long ago without a guardian angel."[19]

In one of our most fascinating interviews, he speculated about life on other planets.

> **Graham:** I think other planets way out there in space, there's plenty of life. But have you ever thought about the fact that we might not recognize life if we saw it? I mean, there are other forms of creation that we possibly cannot sense with our five senses. I was told that by a great scientist, one of the greatest in the world, just the other day.
>
> **Frost:** That we might not recognize life when we see it?
>
> **Graham:** . . . . The Bible speaks of principalities and powers. We know there are demons and angels that we can't see. We know that there are spiritual forces at work in our world that we cannot see. And without the microscope, you would have never seen the germs. There's a form of creation that you'd never see without a modern instrument. And the same is true through the telescope. And we're just on the verge of the most exciting things in the world.

For example, you can go—if you were going to the nearest star to us, it would take an astronaut ten years to get there and back at the speed of light. . . . Now when he got back to the airport here, he would only be ten days older, because when you break the light barrier, as we might break the light barrier by 2000 A.D., time ceases to exist. So that what the Bible teaches about God being from everlasting to everlasting and in the eternal present—everything is before Him; there's no past with God and no future—science now says is absolutely scientifically accurate. There is no time when you break the light barrier.

Frost: That new world, I can see, the world of moon exploration, excites you. Does it worry you that we're reaching a stage where we've got too much control over our environment? I mean, what about when we get to another stage where people will be able to genetically select what their children are like? That's a terrible responsibility, isn't it?

Graham: It is a big responsibility, and these are areas, David, that I wouldn't dare comment on, because—I haven't thought through them. And I'd rather not—I'd be making a statement now that five years from now I'd say, "Oh, I regret that statement I made to David Frost."[20]

Billy Graham has said that the most difficult thing about being famous is that he and his family are "looked at and watched everywhere you go. We live like prisoners. I can't take my children to the beach. I can't take them on a vacation. When my wife and I walk into a country club, people playing cards and drinking get embarrassed or angry. Yet we still go there—Jesus was criticized for mingling with publicans, you know. The greatest thing about going to Russia was the feeling that no one knew you."[21] Once I asked the evangelist about personal security, which is always a concern of people in the public eye, and the Grahams have taken extensive precautions. He told me about their watchdogs.

Frost: Have you ever had an attack made on you or threats on your life?

Graham: David, yes. We have constant threats. As a matter of fact we had about five people in one week . . . [who] tried to get to my home. And most of them are mental cases. And two or three of them the police had to deal with. But we do have this type of thing, so much so that we had to build a fence around my house. Upon security advice, we got three attack dogs. One lives in the house and two on the outside, and they're under complete control; they're trained in Germany. They were given to me by a friend of mine in Philadelphia. . . .

Frost: I'm still terrified about those three dogs of yours. They understand English as well as German, don't they?

Graham: No, they don't. We have to speak to them in German. . . . We have sixteen commands that we give them in German, and if you came to visit us, they'd be very nice. In fact—

Frost: Promise? Promise?

Graham: —One of them would probably lick you to death in welcoming you. But they can change in an instant. Upon a command, and they can become vicious, snarling animals. We've never had to use them, thank the Lord, and I don't think I could ever give a command, no matter what was happening.[22]

Later he added:

> We get [death threats] quite often, and I pay absolutely no
> attention to them. I have no bodyguards, and I don't have
> anybody protecting me like that. And they're just put aside
> and I feel that I'm clothed in the armor of God, and I'll go
> on as long as God wants me to, and if He wants me killed,
> I'm happy to be killed. . . .[23]

Billy Graham is not a man who would seek for monuments, but one place that may honor his ministry as well as any is The Cove, a beautiful retreat center in the mountains of North Carolina where both Ruth and Billy intend to be buried. One of his dreams, he explained, is to turn it "into a place where lay-people can come to study nothing but the Bible—perhaps a speech course on how to teach the Bible or how to witness one-on-one. That's the core of our vision. . . . We hope The Cove will be a place where [people] can go and spend six weeks or a month or a year if necessary and be quiet."[24] Perhaps this is an outgrowth, or expansion, of a dream he had over thirty years ago. In 1964, I asked what he wanted to do with the rest of his life.

> **Graham:** I have probably had ambitions along the lines
> of my work in the sense that I would like to see it expanded
> by the training of other evangelists, and that's what I'm doing
> right now. I'm spending a great deal of my time
> training other evangelists, and I'm trying to get men with
> me who have their earned doctor's degrees from various
> universities.

We have some that are from Britain who have earned their degrees at Oxford and the University of Edinburgh and so forth, and these men are with me now full-time, studying, learning, and are gradually going out on their own, and we have about fifteen evangelists now.

And then I take theological students in the United States to all of our crusades. We have anywhere from 100 to 200 theological students at every crusade studying, and it's almost a traveling theological college, you see, in evangelism. And so, this is my real goal, is to try to train others because I think we're going to need intellectuals in evangelism who can speak to this generation and the future generations.

Frost: Do you see yourself preaching for the rest of your life?

Graham: I didn't see so a few years ago. In fact, I thought after I was here in London and perhaps after I'd been to New York, that interest in my work and my preaching might rather die down, but it seems to have increased, at least in America. And so, I probably will continue carrying on the rest of my life.[25]

His brother-in-law and former colleague Leighton Ford echoed this by saying, "If [Billy] ever stopped preaching, probably he would not be happy. . . . It has been central to him."[26] More recently Billy has said, "The New Testament says nothing of apostles who retired and took it easy."[27]

I wondered what Billy Graham considered as highlights of his life. I know he says marrying Ruth, whom he calls "the most wonderful woman in the whole world," was one of the highlights.[28]

Frost: As you look back over your life, Billy, what would you pick as the highest point, the highest moment, so far?

Graham: I'm not sure that I could do that quickly. I think I would have to say that the time that I gave my life to Christ was the highest, the moment that changed my life irrevocably and made me a new person and gave me a joy and a peace that only Christ can give.

Frost: And have you ever had, since that moment, a moment of doubt?

Graham: Yes. I've had moments of doubt, in the earlier years. I don't have those doubts now. I don't ever doubt that there's a God. I don't ever doubt that the Bible is the Word of God. I don't ever doubt my own personal relationship to Christ. I don't have any doubts about that at all. And I don't doubt that I'm going to heaven when I die.[29]

Endnotes

1. *Donahue*, Interview with Billy Graham, November 1979.
2. "Frost on Sunday: Interview with Billy Graham," TV-am, Great Britain, 1989.
3. "The David Frost Show," Westinghouse Broadcasting, 1969.
4. Myra, Harold. "William Franklin Graham: Seventy Exceptional Years." *Christianity Today*, November 18, 1988, 23.
5. "Doubts and Certainties: David Frost interview with Billy Graham," BBC-2, 1964.
6. *Larry King Live*, Interview with Billy Graham, January 21, 1997.
7. "Reverend Billy Graham talking with David Frost," PBS, January 29, 1993.
8. Cal Thomas on CNBC, February 7, 1995.
9. "Doubts and Certainties: David Frost interview with Billy Graham," BBC-2, 1964.
10. "Reverend Billy Graham talking with David Frost," PBS, January 29, 1993.
11. "The David Frost Show," Westinghouse Broadcasting, 1970.
12. "Graham's View from Japan," *Christianity Today*, February 7, 1994, 47.
13. "Doubts and Certainties: David Frost interview with Billy Graham," BBC-2, 1964.
14. "Reverend Billy Graham talking with David Frost," PBS, January 29, 1993.
15. "Reverend Billy Graham talking with David Frost," PBS, May 30, 1997.
16. Gibbs and Ostling. "God's Billy Pulpit." *Time*, November 15, 1993, 70.
17. *The Today Show*, Interview with Billy Graham, April 1, 1994.
18. Gibbs and Ostling. "God's Billy Pulpit." *Time* , November 15, 1993, 70.
19. *Ibid.*
20. "The David Frost Show," Westinghouse Broadcasting, 1969.
21. "Fame Hasn't Spoiled Billy Graham." *Minneapolis Tribune*, December 12, 1965.
22. "The David Frost Show," Westinghouse Broadcasting, 1970.
23. "Frost on Sunday: Interview with Billy Graham," TV-am, Great Britain, 1989.
24. Myra, Harold. "William Franklin Graham: Seventy Exceptional Years." *Christianity Today*, November 18, 1988, 17.
25. "Doubts and Certainties: David Frost interview with Billy Graham," BBC-2, 1964.
26. Briggs, David. "Graham Heading Into Twilight of Long, Distinguished Career." *Los Angeles Times*, September 21, 1991.
27. Gibbs and Ostling. "God's Billy Pulpit." *Time*, November 15, 1997, 70.
28. *Larry King Live*, Interview with Billy Graham, January 21, 1997.
29. "Reverend Billy Graham talking with David Frost," PBS, January 29, 1993.

CHAPTER 10

Billy Graham
on
End Times and Heaven

For I am persuaded, that neither death, nor life, nor angels, nor principalities, nor powers, nor things present, nor things to come, nor height, nor depth, nor any other creature, shall be able to separate us from the love of God, which is in Christ Jesus our Lord.

The Apostle Paul
Romans 8:38, 39

*A*s I mentioned in the last chapter, early in his ministry, Billy described the heaven he foresaw in colorful details. He said that heaven measured 1,600 square miles and "we are going to sit around the fireplace and have parties, and the angels will wait on us, and we'll drive down the golden streets in a yellow Cadillac convertible."[1] A few years ago, I reminded Billy of his willingness to describe the physical properties of heaven.

> **Frost:** If you look back to those early years in the fifties as an evangelist, what are things that you were saying or doing that you wouldn't do now? I mean, your views have matured in certain ways, haven't they? I remember once you were willing to give the dimensions of heaven, for instance.
>
> **Graham:** Yes. That's right.
>
> **Frost:** You wouldn't do that now?
>
> **Graham:** No. Because I would interpret those passages that I was quoting a little differently today. But there is an indication of it in the Book of Revelation. But I am not a great student of the Book of Revelation though it's a tremendous book and we are told to read it and study it and when we do, we have a special blessing. But I have stuck to what is called the *kerygma*, which is the death, the burial, and the resurrection of Jesus Christ and the fact that people need to repent and come to Christ by faith. And that has been the central core of my message everywhere. And Paul said that he "determined to know nothing among them except Jesus Christ and Him crucified." And I am determined that the cross is my message.[2]

Frost: How would you describe heaven now?

Graham: A place where Christ is. And that's going to be heaven enough for me.

Frost: And hell?

Graham: Hell is going to be a place where Christ is not.[3]

Another time he said, "I believe heaven is a place in which there's no darkness because God is the light. I believe it's a place of total joy and total happiness."[4] And still another description that ranged further afield:

Graham: It will be where Jesus is. And it's going to be filled with people who are perfect. It's going to be a glorious kingdom, but I don't think it's going to be one where we sit down and chat in front of television cameras all the time. It's going to be a place where we work. Of course, this is work, too, but it is going to be a place where we're going to work for God. And He may send us to other planets to help in the redemption of other planets. I don't know.

Frost: And do you think there will turn out to be life on other planets?

Graham: Oh, yes, I think there is life on other planets.

Frost: You think that's why they are there? That they are not . . . as you were saying in your questions just now, it's not purposeless?

Graham: No, I think there's a purpose to it all, and I think there's life on other planets. I don't know what form it takes. I think this is the only planet that Satan landed on and he made this his province. And he's called the "god of this world," "the prince and power of the air." He's given all these names that would indicate that it's this planet that he has, that he has taken over, and we see his footprints everywhere. We pick up our daily newspapers and we see all the terrible things going on. In back of that is this spiritual power of evil that is at work. And, the Bible calls it the "mystery of iniquity." And there's a mystery that I want cleared up myself when I get to heaven.

Frost: I'm sure you will. In fact, you're sure those answers will come when you get to heaven, aren't you?

Graham: Yes, sir. I'm very sure.[5]

"Who will get into heaven?" I inquired. "When you have a God of love, which is the essence of your ministry, won't God have to let everybody into heaven?"

Graham: He doesn't have to do anything if He's God. It's our understanding of God that counts. Is He Who we think He is? He will let everybody into heaven, if they come by the way of the cross. The doors are open to everybody. They can come, but they must come in repentance of their sins and faith in Christ. At least that's the teaching of the New Testament. And there are many other questions at that point that I could raise, you could raise, that we could talk about, because there are questions.

For example, here's a person in the middle of China that's never heard of Jesus. How's he going to get to heaven? I think that there's an answer to that I can even see myself. Because, for example, there were two teachers, both of them from Japan, and they were both Christians, and they were teaching in China just recently and they had gone to Hong Kong and then, they were taking a holiday into the next province and they passed a man that was a beggar.

And he looked like he hadn't had anything to eat in a long time and he was disheveled and he just looked the part of a very hungry man. And one of the girls said, "I think we should speak to him." Now these were Japanese girls. And the other one said, "No, let's go on." So they went on.

When they came back, the man was still there and so their conscience began to speak to them. So they went over and they spoke to him about God. And he said, "You know, I have thought about Him all my life, but I didn't know His name." And he said, "I pray to Him, but don't know anything about Him." So they told him all about Jesus and about God and the tears would come down his cheeks. And he said, "I've had a longing to know this all my life, but no one ever told me before."

And I think there is that hunger for God and people are living as best they know how according to the light that they have. Well, I think they're in a separate category than people like Hitler and people who have just defied God, and shaken their fists at God.

Frost: So there is some sort of "holding pattern" or purgatory where the person who never had a chance to know God can, as it were, pass the test into heaven?

Graham: I wouldn't call it purgatory and I wouldn't even call it a "holding pattern." I would say that God, being a God of mercy, we have to rest it right there, and say that God is a God of mercy and love, and how it happens, we don't know. I'm not going to go beyond the teachings of the Scripture.

Frost: But if God is the sort of God you say He is, He'll take care of that?

Graham: He'll take over. And He won't make any mistakes. There's not going to be anybody in hell that wasn't

supposed to be there and there's not going to be anybody
in heaven that wasn't supposed to be there. And I'll leave it
at that. And, then there are people that say that hell is not
eternal, and so forth. I leave all that in God's hands.[6]

Repeatedly Billy has said he looks forward to death. An interesting
aspect of that is what he says is his greatest fear: ". . . that I'll do
something or say something that will bring some disrepute on the
Gospel of Christ before I go. And I want the Lord to remove me
before I say something or do something that would embarrass God."[7]

"You told me that you are looking forward to death," I said to
Billy. "Why?"

> **Graham:** I would like to die today if it weren't for
> responsibilities that I think God has given me. I'm looking
> forward to going to heaven. That's going to be a great occa-
> sion, and I'm looking forward to seeing Christ face-to-face
> and seeing old friends again and living the life that the Bible
> describes so beautifully in a place where there will never be
> war and hatred and the prejudices that we have here, and
> then serving Him. We're told that we're going to be servants.
> He may send me to another planet somewhere to preach the
> Gospel. I hope so.
>
> **Frost:** Well, I hope to interview you there, too.
>
> **Graham:** Thank you. I surely hope you will, David.[8]

Billy has related close calls with death that he's had, including
a very frightening trip on the Concorde, when an engine blew up.
He admits he was tense and nervous at the time. A flight attendant

asked him to pray for her. Billy says, "I held her hand, and other people gathered around, and I prayed out loud that if it was God's will that He spare us and take us safely back."[9] Why the fear since he knows he is going to heaven? "I have perfect peace about my future. Of course, I have the natural tensions and fears of self-preservation, because if we didn't have them we might walk in front of a truck or something else. So that when a plane gets in a thunderstorm, I grip the seat just like anybody else, but that's not because I'm afraid."[10]

Perhaps this is why Billy told me we need to discuss death more than we do—because we are all going to die.

Graham: We face death every day. We see it in the papers and so forth, people dying, people that we see on the screens later in their motion pictures that we know they're dead now. And we have tried in this generation, in my judgment, to suppress death like the nineteenth-century people tried to suppress sex. We today are in the process of suppressing discussions of death and life after death.

The night that we watched that terrible spectacle of Bobby Kennedy, Senator Bobby Kennedy, on the floor of the Ambassador Hotel, lying there in a pool of blood, and we saw this fellow that carried dishes come and put a religious object in his hand, and they say that the last conscious thing that Bobby Kennedy ever did was to close his hand. Now the thing that meant more to Senator Kennedy at that moment was not the fact that he'd just won the California primary, not the fact that he had all of this prominence and wealth and power. It was his relationship to God and it was the fact that he was staring eternity in the face.

And yet we don't prepare for that. How many universities

today take up the subject of death and life after death as something to be discussed? And if you listen, though, to the folk music that our young people are singing, a lot of it's about death. Our young people want to know about it, but we're not telling them anything about it. We're trying to suppress it. And I think we ought to bring it out in the open. . . . How many television shows do you ever watch in which death is discussed and what happens after death?

I believe . . . that there is an actual, literal heaven. I believe there's an actual, literal hell. I—don't ask me where and don't ask me what it's going to look like and all of that. I don't know. I only know that Jesus warned us about one and told us the joys and the happiness of the other.

Frost: Is there any sort of material example you could give of what heaven would be like? I mean, people sometimes talk about paradise and they say it's like a beautiful piece of music by Beethoven. Is there any symbol that you use?

Graham: Well, see, a lot of people don't like Beethoven. . . . And I think that everything for our personal happiness will be there, and the Scripture says a very interesting thing, that we're going to serve Him. We're not going to just sit down under a palm tree and have a pretty girl wave a palm leaf over us.

Frost: Now, that would attract me about heaven . . .

Graham: We're going to work there. Now, maybe that wouldn't attract you, but with all that you're doing, I'd rather think it might, because there's going to be plenty of work. And when you think of the fact that there are 100 billion galaxies outside of our own galaxy, there's plenty of room up there for a lot of work and a lot of achievement, and I think we're going to travel from planet to planet. It's going to be a marvelous world in the future.

Frost: Where is hell? What are the people in hell going to be doing?

Graham: Well, I don't know. I don't ever expect to find out. But I'll tell you this: I deserve judgment, and I deserve hell, because of my sin. Because all of us are sinners. We're rebels against God. I'm going to be in heaven, and the password to heaven is going to be the grace of God, the fact that God loves me and He says, "I give you eternal life as a gift." It's free. And I'm going there by the grace of God in Christ.[11]

In another context, Billy had said that from a humanist point of view man has a very pessimistic future. "But we have to take into account God. God is not going to allow man to destroy himself on this planet because before that time Christ is going to come back and set up His kingdom. To the Jew He's the Messiah, to the Christian, it's Jesus Christ."[12]

Billy's also said, "The Bible has a tremendous program for the future that God has outlined. God's not going to leave us dangling; He's not going to let us blow ourselves into oblivion and destruction. God has a plan and yet we don't study it, we don't preach it. The average Christian of today is totally ignorant of that Book."[13] So I asked, "When do you believe Christ will come again?"

Graham: I don't know, because when the disciples asked Jesus that very question, He said, "I don't know, and it's not for you to know. Only My Father knows." Only God knows the answer to that. I personally think the way the world is moving and the signs that He left us are converging at one point for the first time in history. I think that His coming may be relatively soon. Now, by "relatively," I'm not sure in your lifetime or mine, but certainly it's nearer now than when he made the prediction 2,000 years ago.

Frost: Good prediction. Before you go, just tell me what do you know of what will happen then? What are you led to believe will happen when He comes again?

Graham: Before He comes again the world is going to go through many convulsions, the Bible teaches. There will be worldwide lawlessness. There will be an overemphasis on sex. There will be an acceleration in technology. He said, "As it was in the days of Noah." There will be a falling away from the church. There are about twenty-seven signs that He left.

Frost: Well, that list makes it sound like tomorrow.

Graham: That's the reason that I say "relatively soon." And I can only go so far as to repeat: sooner than when He made the prediction.

Frost: But what will happen then?

Graham: He will come and He's going to set up His kingdom. The ships will still sail the sea. The trains will still run. The planes will still be in the air. And all the things that science is now getting a glimpse of will all come true. Man will live for 1,000 years. Death will be eliminated. The lion and the lamb will lie down together. The black children and white children of Alabama will walk hand in hand. And it's going to be a marvelous world—the utopia that people have dreamed of is going to be brought. There will be social justice, racial justice. There'll be no war. There'll be no police forces. We won't need police forces. No crime. It's going to be a marvelous world ruled by one Man—Jesus Christ. And the whole earth and the new heavens will be renovated, and the Bible tells about the New Jerusalem coming down, and the heaven and the twenty-first and twenty-second chapter of the Book of Revelation gives vivid descriptions of what heaven is going to be like.[14]

"Is peace on earth impossible?" I wondered.

Graham: The peace that Christ really came to bring was personal peace—peace of the individual in the midst of a turmoiled world and a frustrated, confused, warring world. "My peace I give unto you," He said. And also He came to bring peace on earth in the sense that peace with God—you see, this planet is looked upon in the Bible as at war with God. He came to bring peace between man and God. And then, thirdly, He came to bring ultimate peace. There is going to be peace on earth. I mean, we're going to have a world peace. There's no doubt, but it's not going to be brought about by Mr. U Thant in the United Nations. They're going to try, and they can patch it up here and there, but it's going to break out all over.

The only permanent peace the world will ever know is when God intervenes in human history and Jesus Christ is put on the throne, and He's going to rule and reign, and we're going to have peace. But He will rule with a rod of iron, the Bible says. And that is when death will be eliminated, suffering will be eliminated, poverty eliminated.

Frost: Last time, the first coming of Christ, He came to Palestine. Is there any indication of which country He might come to next time?

Graham: Oh, the fourteenth chapter of Zachariah tells us exactly where He's coming to.

Frost: Oh, I'd forgotten the fourteenth chapter.

Graham: He's going to come on the Mount of Olives. He's going to stand on the Mount of Olives, the Bible says.

And the Bible teaches that Jerusalem will become the capital of the world, and from Jerusalem Christ is going to reign.[15]

Once, when asked who he wanted to preach his funeral, Billy joked, "I might preach it myself and put it on tape and let people see me preach my own funeral. Then I'd tell some things that they never knew before."[16] Thankfully, we don't yet have that sermon. However, I asked him how he'd like to be remembered.

Frost: What would you like the first line of your obituary to say?

Graham: Well, I suppose that "He was faithful," and that "He had integrity." Because the psalmist said, "I walk in my integrity," and I would like to be considered a person who had integrity, and who was faithful to his calling, and who loved God with all his heart, mind, and soul.

Frost: You're obviously going to heaven, aren't you?

Graham: Well, I'm going to heaven, not on my good works, or because I've preached to all these people or read the Bible. I'm going to heaven because of what Christ did on the cross.[17]

Endnotes

1. Gibbs and Ostling. "God's Billy Pulpit." *Time*, November 15, 1993.

2. "Reverend Billy Graham Talking with David Frost," PBS, January 29, 1993.

3. "A Prophet with Honor: David Frost documentary on Billy Graham," Channel Four, Great Britain, 1989.

4. *Larry King Live*, Interview with Billy Graham, January 21, 1997.

5. "Reverend Billy Graham talking with David Frost," PBS, January 29, 1993.

6. *Ibid.*

7. *CBS This Morning*, Interview with Billy Graham, September 23, 1991.

8. "A Prophet with Honor: David Frost documentary on Billy Graham," Channel Four, Great Britain, 1989.

9. *Larry King Live*, Interview with Billy Graham, January 21, 1997.

10. "Billy Graham, the Man at Home." *The Saturday Evening Post*, Spring 1972.

11. "The David Frost Show," Westinghouse Broadcasting, 1969.

12. *Donahue*, Interview with Billy Graham, October 11, 1979.

13. Wakin, Edward. "Revival Tents and Golden Domes." *U.S. Catholic*, March 1976.

14. "The David Frost Show," Westinghouse Broadcasting, 1969.

15. "The David Frost Show," Westinghouse Broadcasting, 1970.

16. Cal Thomas on CNBC, February 7, 1995.

17. "Reverend Billy Graham talking with David Frost," PBS, January 29, 1993.

EPILOGUE

May 30, 1997

Frost: I hope this is not our last interview. But, if this were to be our last interview, what is the message you would most want to communicate at the end of it?

Graham: That God loves you. I tell people in every crusade we hold, "If you forget everything that happens in this crusade, remember one thing, God loves you." Because God does love you. No matter what you've done or what you've said or been, He loves you. And that love is impossible for us to describe, because He uses totally different terminology to describe it in the Greek language, to describe God's love. And then when God's love comes into our hearts, that too is supernatural. There are some people that maybe you wouldn't normally love, but He gives you the power to love that person. And I can say to you right now, that I just—I love everybody. I don't have any people I don't like or dislike. I just accept everybody.

Frost: Well, could we—why don't we close with prayer?

Graham: That would be wonderful. Our Father, we thank Thee for this time together. We thank Thee for the many times we have had in the past. We pray that Thou wouldst bless David and his family. And we pray that Thou wouldst bless the country from which He comes, where we have spent so much time. Thank You for all the friends we have there. We pray that Thou wouldst bless the leadership there. And we pray for the whole world in the same way. May this be a period of peace. And as we enter the twenty-first century, may it be a time of peace, if it be Thy will. Lord, bring us together, we pray Thee, in Jesus name. Amen.

Billy Graham:

A Chronology

*A*s I look back over Billy's life and our conversations, the following dates and events stand out to me as some of the most important and memorable.

November 7, 1918
Born into a North Carolina farm family.

1936
Graduates from high school and becomes a Fuller Brush salesman.

Enrolls in Bob Jones College in Tennessee.

1937
Transfers to Florida Bible Institute.

Preaches first sermon at Bostwick Baptist Church in Florida.

1938
Commits himself to God and preaching.

Holds first revival, at the East Palatka Baptist Church in Florida.

1940

Graduates and is voted outstanding evangelist at Florida Bible Institute.

Enrolls at Wheaton College in Wheaton, Illinois, where he meets Ruth Bell.

1943

Marries Ruth Bell.

Assumes pastorate of Western Springs Baptist Church in suburban Chicago.

1944

Launches radio broadcast career with "Songs in the Night," and is joined by George Beverly Shea, who sings at crusade services throughout Graham's ministry.

Preaches to his first mass rally in Chicago for Youth for Christ.

1945

Becomes full-time evangelist with Youth for Christ

1947

Attracts 42,000 people to a Charlotte, North Carolina, rally, marking the first time his team works together.

Becomes president of Northwestern Schools, in Minneapolis, Minnesota, but spends little time there.

1948

Agrees with his team to the "Modesto Manifesto," guidelines for handling temptations that had brought down evangelists in the past.

1949

Raises his profile during a Los Angeles, California, crusade, in part because of newspaperman William Randolph Hearst's order to "puff Graham."

1950

Begins "Hour of Decision" radio program and World Wide Pictures to produce documentaries and evangelism-oriented fiction films.

Visits President Truman in the White House, his first presidential visit.

1953

Publishes first book, *Peace with God.*

Resigns from Northwestern Schools to concentrate on crusades, which are booming.

Bans seating discrimination at his rallies, carefully calling for more racial inclusion.

1954

Attracts two million people in twelve weeks to Harringay Arena, his first London crusade, winning over skeptical clergy and journalists.

1956

Establishes *Christianity Today* magazine.

1957

Accepts an invitation from liberal Protestants to hold crusade in New York City, breaking with fundamentalists. "Evangelical" begins to take on separate identity from "fundamentalist."

1958

Steps up pressure against racial discrimination in a rally on the lawn of the South Carolina statehouse.

1963

Draws over 134,000 to a rally at the Coliseum in Los Angeles.

Declines to take part in the civil rights "March on Washington" because the movement is moving "too far too fast."

1964

David Frost first interviews Graham on BBC-2.

1967

Preaches in Communist Yugoslavia and is warmly received in Italy by Roman Catholic and Greek Orthodox clergy.

1969

David Frost interviews Billy on "The David Frost Show."

Preaches at first White House church service launched by newly inaugurated President Nixon.

1970

David Frost interviews Billy on "The David Frost Show."

1972

Meets with President Nixon and maintains regular contact with his reelection campaign.

Meets with all parties in Northern Ireland, including the IRA, in attempt to diffuse violence.

1973

Holds first crusade in South Africa, which is the first major public interracial gathering in that nation.

Preaches to 1,120,000 in Korea for the largest public religious service in history.

1974

Draws Protestant evangelical leaders from 150 nations for conference in Lausanne, Switzerland.

Watches from a distance as Watergate brings President Nixon down.

1977

Skips President Carter's inauguration after staying away from presidential race; first inauguration he's missed since 1949.

1978

Travels to Poland and is inspired to preach more on peace and reconciliation after visiting Auschwitz.

1979

Influences founding of the Evangelical Council for Financial Accountability, credited with opening and cleaning up of parachurch groups' finances.

1981

Meets Pope John II at the Vatican.

Ministers at President Reagan's bedside after the President is shot.

1982

Preaches for first time in Russia.

1983

Receives the Presidential Medal of Freedom from President Reagan, the nation's highest civilian honor.

1987

Opens the Billy Graham Training Center at The Cove, a retreat set in the North Carolina mountains near his home.

1988

Preaches in China, fulfilling a dream of his wife, who was born there.

1989

David Frost both interviews and airs a documentary on Billy.

1990

Joins *Life* magazine's list of "The 100 Most Important Americans of the Twentieth Century."

1991

Joins President Bush at the White House during the launch of the war against Iraq.

Hosts nearly 5,000 pastors and church workers attending his five-day School of Evangelism in Moscow.

1993

David Frost interviews Graham on PBS.

Gathers 3,900 evangelists from around the world for a conference in Amsterdam.

1995

Applauds the Southern Baptist Convention for its resolution apologizing for slavery and condemning racism.

Collapses in Toronto and is hospitalized; is told to lighten his schedule.

Announces his son Franklin will take over his ministry after he dies.

1996

Reaches out to the MTV generation, mixing pop music and interviews with his preaching, in a program that goes out in forty-eight languages to 160 countries.

Receives the Congressional Gold Medal, along with Ruth, at the Capitol Rotunda.

1997

Publishes his long-awaited memoir, *Just as I Am.*
David Frost interviews Graham on PBS.

Just As I Am

Billy Graham's memoirs
is available from HarperCollins Publishers.